THE MEDITERRANEAN SLOW COOKER COOKBOOK

THE MEDITERRANEAN SLOW COOKER COOKBOOK

A Mediterranean Diet Cookbook with 101 Easy Slow Cooker Recipes

SALINAS PRESS

Contents

Introduction

Welcome to the delights of slow-cooked goodness—Mediterranean style. Brimming with their distinct cultural and culinary histories, the countries that border the Mediterranean Sea, including Greece, Italy, France, Spain, and Morocco, have long been associated with signature flavors and ingredients that are known for being both healthful and delicious. Mediterranean cuisine calls to mind colorful dishes featuring fresh local fish, heart-healthy olive oil, and just-picked produce, accompanied by some good local wine.

The recipes in *The Mediterranean Slow Cooker Cookbook* help you make dishes that bear the hallmarks of this vibrant, healthful cuisine. Offering wondrous, deep flavors, these recipes are made using simple ingredients that can be prepared with little fuss. In fact, one of the things you'll notice right away is that the recipes in the book call for easy-to-find ingredients.

If you're new to Mediterranean-style cooking, you'll quickly discover that cooking these dishes is really simple. You just keep a few key ingredients on hand in your refrigerator and pantry. The recipes also require very little preparation time—usually less than 15 minutes. And the best part? The experts agree, Mediterranean-style cuisine is very healthful. While the recipes in this book are not specifically designed for weight loss, they may lead to that extra benefit because of their nutritious ingredients.

With the book, you'll soon master techniques that combine the ease of slow cooking with the desirable foods and flavors for which Mediterranean cuisine is known. One of the unique things about cooking with a slow cooker is the resulting flavor. You can toss all sorts of items into your cooker to simmer all day long and get incredible results. Meats cook slowly in their own juices, allowing them to tenderize and make the most of their inherent flavors. Even the tougher varieties of vegetables can be cooked to tender perfection in a slow cooker. And who knew decadently rich desserts can be made even better in a slow cooker?

The opening chapter provides information on how to get the most out of your slow cooker as well as explaining the key benefits of this tried-and-true cooking method. Included are practical cooking techniques, handy tips for using and maintaining your slow cooker, safety tips, and a reference chart for converting cooking times of your favorite conventional recipes to slow cooker times. Chapter Two discusses the many foods and ingredients commonly associated with Mediterranean cuisine, including regional flavor profiles that characterize this style of cooking. A useful list of foods and ingredients lets you easily set up and maintain your own well-stocked Mediterranean kitchen.

The rest of the book's chapters present a delicious array of more than 100 recipes you will want to try immediately—all easily cooked in the slow cooker. You'll find examples of the most mouthwatering types of Mediterranean cuisine, from tasty soups and pastas, hearty grains, and delicious vegetables, to fresh and flavorful seafood, poultry, and meats— all topped off by sinfully good desserts that will satisfy your sweet tooth.

With this essential guide in hand, you'll soon be on your way to slow cooking the many Mediterranean-style dishes you enjoy, and bringing them to your table.

CHAPTER ONE

Getting the Most Out of Your Slow Cooker

Cooking food long, low, and slow is one of the best ways to attain deep, satisfying flavors. Slow cooking can be accomplished using dry heat, as in a roaster or the oven, or using moist heat, which is the basis of cooking with an electric slow cooker. As food cooks in a sealed ceramic slow-cooker pot and steam accumulates , the condensation collecting inside the crock acts as an efficient baster, leading to extremely juicy, tender meats, vegetables, and other ingredients.

Using a slow cooker is one of the easiest ways to introduce healthy home cooking into even the busiest of lifestyles. You can generally put the desired ingredients in your slow cooker and return hours later or at the end of the day to a delicious, ready-to-eat meal. Even if you've never used a slow cooker before, you can quickly become a slow cooking pro! And why wouldn't you? There are many benefits to this style of cooking, some of which may even surprise you.

BENEFITS OF SLOW COOKING

In today's fast-paced world, using a slow cooker lets you economize your time and effort in the kitchen. Often, the first reason people reach for slow cookers is that they are easy to use and they save so much time. The recipes in this book are quick and easy to prepare, a key to ease in the kitchen and a necessity when working around a packed schedule. Many of the recipes will allow you to simply fill your slow cooker with ingredients and go—this is especially true with soups and stews.

This style of cooking lets you plan ahead and have the option to leave your morning free. If you're short on time in the morning, do your prep work the night before and refrigerate ingredients overnight. This way you can simply assemble the ingredients in the slow cooker pot in the morning, turn it on, and head out the door. Just remember: when you wake up, take the ingredients out of the refrigerator to reach room temperature before cooking.

Using a slow cooker is one of the best ways to cook the least expensive cuts of meat, letting you cut costs without sacrificing flavor. Beef brisket, chicken thighs, lamb shoulder, and pork shoulder are all great examples of meats that come out tender, juicy, and flavorful after slow cooking but are difficult to prepare successfully otherwise. You can also use less meat in slow cooker recipes because the long simmering brings out the most of the meaty flavor and lets it infuse the whole dish. This in turn allows you to fortify your dishes with vegetables, pastas, whole grains, and beans, in keeping with Mediterranean tradition, while still maintaining a savory, meaty taste.

TIPS AND TECHNIQUES FOR USING YOUR SLOW COOKER

One key to getting great results time after time with a slow cooker is preparation. That doesn't mean you need to spend a lot of time up front. Just incorporate a few simple habits into your preparation and cooking routine when following or adapting a recipe for a slow cooker. The following tips and techniques will help you maximize your results every time. Plus, you'll have fun making picture-perfect dishes that will impress your family and friends.

Use the right tools. Use plastic, rubber, or wooden utensils when stirring foods in your glazed ceramic slow cooker or serving dishes from it. Use a soft sponge to clean the cooker since metal utensils and scouring pads can scratch the surface of the crock (see additional cleaning tips on page 7).

Cut food evenly. Especially when dealing with denser vegetables that are more difficult to cook through, such as carrots, potatoes, or yams, be sure to cut the food into pieces of about the same size. This will ensure that they cook at a similar rate, so you can avoid mushy pieces and underdone pieces in the same dish.

Brown food first as needed. At times—when you are able or when the recipe specifically calls for it—you will want to brown certain foods first to enhance flavor. Onions browned beforehand have a different flavor from those put into the slow cooker raw. You may want to experiment, as you might find you prefer one or the other in different recipes. You also may prefer to brown meat for some recipes to give it color and flavor, but generally this is not essential. If you do choose to brown meat or poultry in advance for your recipe, do so by placing a small amount of olive oil in a nonstick skillet large enough to accommodate the meat or poultry. Warm the oil over medium-high heat on the stove until shimmering, and brown the meat or poultry evenly on all sides, in small batches if necessary.

Don't use frozen foods in slow cooker recipes. To maintain food safety, your slow cooker must reach a temperature of at least 140°F in 4 hours or less. A prolonged cooking process at inadequate temperatures increases the likelihood that harmful bacteria will grow in your food. Always thaw frozen vegetables, as directed, and before you add them to the slow cooker. Take special care with larger pieces of meat and poultry, which should be thawed in the refrigerator a day or two before cooking.

Go easy on the liquid. Because your slow cooker will have a tightly sealed lid, little or no evaporation occurs during cooking, and this cooking method releases the juices from the other ingredients. Use only enough liquid to make the recipe work. The liquid should just cover the other ingredients. Be careful not to overfill your slow cooker, or liquid might leak out of the top. This will not only make a mess but will prevent the food from cooking as it should. Ideally, your slow cooker should be one-half to two-thirds full and no more than three-quarters full. If adapting a recipe that wasn't written for slow cookers, reduce the liquid by about one-third. And use the liquid to its full advantage: Rather than water, opt for flavorful liquids like fruit juice, chicken stock, seafood stock, vegetable juice, vegetable stock, and wine. Since the liquid won't evaporate, a little will go a long way.

Use fats sparingly. One of the best things about using a slow cooker is that you can really cut down on the amount of fat in your dishes. The moisture inside the sealed crock prevents foods from sticking to the inside of the crock, so you don't need to add oil for that purpose to any of your recipes. Cooking meat on the stove top causes the fat to drain away, but it can't drain out of a slow cooker. Too much fat will result in an unpleasant texture in the final meal, so keep fat to a minimum or eliminate it entirely. Remove skin from chicken and trim excess fat from meat. The flavor of your food won't suffer. And, of course, it goes without saying that less fat means more healthful results.

Use a simple homemade paste to thicken or reduce sauces. Since the liquid in your slow cooker doesn't evaporate, it also doesn't thicken or reduce in the traditional sense. To counteract this problem, simply coat the meat in your recipe in a small amount of flour, sea salt, and black pepper before adding it to the slow cooker, which will thicken the drippings and liquid. If a dish doesn't have meat or it isn't the kind of meat you'd like to coat, use a little cornstarch toward the end of the cooking time: Mix 1 or 2 teaspoons with a small amount of cold water to form a paste, turn up the cooker to high, and then stir the paste into the liquid as it simmers. The liquid will thicken in a few minutes.

Use seasonings liberally. Slow cooking requires more of your usual herbs and spices so their flavors can survive the lengthy cooking process. If using dried herbs, use a bit more than you normally would. Use fresh herbs liberally, but if possible, do not add them until the last 60 minutes of cooking. Season the dish with sea salt and black pepper. Be prepared to taste and adjust seasoning again before you serve the meal. A special note about beans: When you cook with dried beans, never salt them before they're cooked to the point of being almost tender. If you add salt too soon, it toughens the outer coating of the bean and inhibits proper cooking.

Arrange your ingredients carefully in the slow cooker. Many recipes provide a specific order in which ingredients should be added to the crock, so follow the steps closely. Typically, vegetables cook more slowly than meats and should go at the bottom of the pot. Root vegetables can take longer than meat and other vegetables, so be sure to put these near the heat source, at the bottom of the pot.

Add certain foods toward the end of cooking time. Tender vegetables, fresh herbs, dairy products, pasta, and seafood require much less cooking time than most other foods. For that reason, plan to add them to your slow cooker toward the end of the cooking time. Vegetables that are cooked too long can turn out mushy. Herbs that are overcooked lose their flavor. Pasta, if cooked too long, can even disintegrate. Seafood that gets too much time in the slow cooker can be tough or even inedible. And be especially careful when slow cooking with dairy products. Too much time in the cooker causes liquid dairy products like milk and cream to curdle, and aged cheese to become oily. Add fresh dairy products during the last 60 minutes of cooking. If that isn't an option and the recipe is appropriate for substitution, use canned sweetened condensed milk or evaporated milk.

Keep the lid closed during cooking. Your slow cooker relies upon the tight seal of the lid to help maintain its steam-condensation cycle. When adding ingredients, or if you must check on your food or stir it, do it quickly. Each time you lift off the lid, heat and moisture escape from your slow cooker, and it can take up to 20 minutes to recover the full amount of heat lost. This makes the cooking take longer, and your existing time cycle may not be sufficient.

Choose the right temperature setting for your needs. The cooker has two temperature settings: low and high. Low is 200°F and high is 300°F. Both settings cook meat safely. Since food becomes more flavorful the longer it simmers in its own juices, choose the low setting whenever possible for the best taste. This is also the best setting if you plug it in before you go off to work. You won't have to give the slow cooker another thought during your busy day. Choose the high setting when you want a meal in a few hours, rather than at the end of the day. The food will still be delicious, just not quite as flavorful as after an all-day simmer. It's useful to remember that 1 hour on high is equal to about 2½ hours on low. The handy chart at the end of this chapter can help you navigate between the high and low settings to suit your schedule. If a recipe suggests cooking your stew on low for 7 hours, but you want to eat it in 3 hours, just set the slow cooker on high.

Avoid using your crock for food storage. Even when you prep ingredients the night before, store them in a different container. Refrigerating and/or freezing the crock (and then returning it to room temperature and heating it) can cause it to crack.

Slow cookers are not intended for reheating food. Use your slow cooker to make mouthwateringly good meals; use your oven, stove, toaster oven, or microwave to reheat leftovers—if there are any.

WASHING YOUR SLOW COOKER

With proper care, your slow cooker will last for several years. Follow these simple guidelines to keep your slow cooker clean and in good working order:

- Always unplug the slow cooker before cleaning to avoid the risk of electrical shock.
- If your slow cooker is new or you haven't used it in a while, wash each part of it separately.
- Do not immerse the metal housing and base in water, because they can be damaged or cause a hazard.
- Use a clean, soapy cloth or sponge to wash the inside of the slow cooker pot. Metal utensils or scouring pads will scratch it.
- Most removable cooking crocks and lids can be washed in the dishwasher. Plastic lids should be loaded on the top rack of the dishwasher to prevent warping.
- After washing, dry the slow cooker well with a soft cloth.

SLOW COOKER SAFETY

When using a slow cooker, it's important to remember a few facts about temperature and bacteria. Your slow cooker must reach a temperature of at least 140°F in 4 hours or less, which is essential to the maintenance of food safety. Any prolonged cooking process at inadequate temperatures increases the risk of harmful bacteria breeding in your food. For these reasons, power outages should be treated with care. If your power was out for under 2 hours, you may resume cooking. Your alternative is to remove the ingredients from the crock and finish cooking using a more conventional method, such as the stove top or oven. If the outage was 2 hours or longer, the food must be discarded to avoid food-borne illnesses.

You already know that pre-browning can have aesthetic and savory value, but browning ingredients before they go into the cooker also has a food-safety benefit. The danger zone for growth of harmful bacteria is between 40°F and 140°F. This means if the food has been warmer than refrigerator temperature but cooler than very hot tap water temperature for too long, it is in danger of becoming a breeding ground for bacteria. By browning meats in advance, you kill any bacteria on the surface of the food. Then once the slow cooking process begins and proceeds, the cooking process eliminates any remaining bacteria.

A final note on extreme temperatures and the ceramic cooking crock and glass lid (if the lid isn't plastic): These parts of a slow cooker can crack or break as they react to dramatic changes in temperature. If very cold ingredients are added when these parts are very hot, or if the parts are placed on very cold surfaces, they may break.

Slow cooking is not only easy, but safe, as long as you are mindful of these simple precautionary measures. Always use common sense, and err on the side of caution if you are in doubt.

COOKING TIME CONVERSIONS

Use this chart to convert traditional cooking times to the length of time to cook foods in your slow cooker. If cooking on the high setting, you may want to check for doneness a couple of hours before reaching the longest estimated cooking time, but remember that lifting the lid allows heat and moisture to escape from your slow cooker and can extend the cooking time.

Conventional Cooking Times	High Setting	Low Setting
15 to 30 minutes	1 to 2 hours	4 to 6 hours
30 minutes to 1 hour	2 to 3 hours	5 to 7 hours
1 to 2 hours	3 to 4 hours	6 to 8 hours
2 to 4 hours	4 to 6 hours	8 to 12 hours

NOTE: IF COOKING AT ALTITUDES OF 4,000 FEET OR MORE, YOU'LL NEED TO INCREASE THE COOKING TIME BY 40 TO 50 PERCENT.

CHAPTER TWO

Your Mediterranean Kitchen

If you are even lightly acquainted with Mediterranean-style cooking, you can probably guess that its emphasis on fresh, traditional foods readily supports healthful eating practices. Whether you are actively seeking to eat healthier, hoping to enhance an already healthy lifestyle, looking for new and flavorful dishes to try, or seeking ways to save time and still enjoy home-cooked meals—or a combination of all of these reasons—with a little planning, it's a cinch to set up and maintain your own Mediterranean kitchen. The information and handy pantry lists in this chapter will help you get organized and will make the transition in your own kitchen simple.

WHAT IS MEDITERRANEAN CUISINE?

Although nowadays touted as a modern way of eating, Mediterranean cuisine is rooted in traditional practices of the diverse countries bordering the deep, azure sea "between the lands" that gives the cuisine its moniker. The flavorful foods of Greece, Italy, Morocco, Southern France, and Spain readily come to mind as representative of this style of eating, often praised for its inherently healthful aspects. If the idea of cooking and eating Mediterranean dishes seems exotic or difficult to accomplish, don't be the least bit daunted. The basic foods and ingredients needed to stock your Mediterranean kitchen can be easily obtained at most major grocery stores.

The colors and flavors of Mediterranean cuisine signal the broad range of vitamins and other nutrients it provides. This cuisine is generally defined by a very high proportion of fruits, vegetables, legumes, whole grains, and olive oil; a relatively high proportion of seafood; a moderate proportion of dairy products; moderate wine consumption; and proportionately lower amounts of other lean meats.

When meal planning and choosing which recipes to try, aim to include fruits, vegetables, and whole grains in most of your meals. Fruits, vegetables, pasta, beans, and minimally processed whole grains make up the largest proportion of the Mediterranean cuisine and will lend substance and flavor to the Mediterranean-style dishes you prepare in your slow cooker.

Healthful fats are also a major component of this now popular cuisine. Olives and olive oil are staples of Mediterranean cooking; nuts and seeds are also high-quality sources of healthful fats, fiber, and protein. Unprocessed, natural cheeses, yogurt, and milk are an important part of Mediterranean cuisine, although in more modest proportion than, for example, the vegetable, fruit, legume, and whole grain groups.

As for protein, Mediterranean cuisine is full of choices. Fish and shellfish provide excellent protein and healthful fats when following a Mediterranean diet. Eggs offer high-quality protein, particularly for vegetarians. Lean, unprocessed meats are also sources of protein in this style of cooking and eating.

FLAVOR PROFILES OF MEDITERRANEAN REGIONS

You will discover several basic flavor profiles within Mediterranean cuisine, each corresponding to a region or country and containing several signature flavors. Getting to know these flavor combinations will help you improvise as well as keep the right ingredients on hand for the Mediterranean dishes you want to make on a regular basis. Here are some well-known Mediterranean flavor profiles to keep in mind, along with some time-saver tips if you're pressed for time.

Regions: **Southern France and Southern Italy**

Flavor Profile: **anchovy, garlic, olive oil, parsley, and tomato**

Time-saver tips:

Anchovy paste is an instant way to add flavor to recipes. Sold packaged in tubes, it can be kept in the refrigerator for months.

Parsley paste is made with olive oil and garlic in addition to fresh parsley and is an excellent way to capture this flavor profile instantly. Also sold in tubes, it too can be refrigerated for extended periods of time.

Region: **Northern Italy**

Flavor Profile: **garlic, red wine vinegar, white wine vinegar, and wine**

Time-saver tip:

Fresh minced garlic is sold in jars in the produce section of most markets, letting you avoid peeling and mincing garlic yourself when you are in a hurry.

Region: **Spain**

Flavor Profile: **almonds, bell pepper, garlic, hazelnuts, olive oil, onion, pine nuts, tomato, and walnuts**

Time-saver tips:

Chopped nuts, available at most grocers, take the chore of shelling and prepping out of your hands.

Chopped onion is readily accessible and will help you avoid chopping and onion tears.

Region: **Morocco**

Flavor Profile: **apricots, cinnamon, coriander, cumin, dates, figs, ginger, onion, raisins, and tomato**

Time-saver tips:

Fresh ginger is sold in crushed, minced, and paste form—very handy because the root itself requires time-consuming peeling and preparation.

Diced tomatoes can be found fresh or canned at grocery stores if you wish to save on preparation time.

Region: **Greece**

Flavor Profile: **cinnamon, cucumber, strained yogurt, and tomato**

- -

Time-saver tip:

Greek yogurt is the right kind of yogurt to keep on hand because it is strained. Look for the plain variety in whatever fat content you prefer.

- -

SETTING UP YOUR MEDITERRANEAN PANTRY

Keeping a Mediterranean pantry is a simple, practical matter of planning how to stock your refrigerator, freezer, pantry, and spice rack. Start modestly and expand your Mediterranean pantry as you add new dishes to your repertoire, or go wild and set it up all at once. Whatever your style, keeping some or all of these ingredients on hand will simplify creating quick meals and improvising.

What to Keep in Your Refrigerator

Fresh fruits and vegetables are central to Mediterranean cuisine, so this is a good place to start. Naturally, this means that you may need to shop more frequently than you have in the past to maintain a good supply of fresh produce. Keep a list handy—magnetized refrigerator notepads are great for this—so you'll have a note for what items to pick up as you're coming and going. If traveling to the grocery store or market is a longer journey for you, consider investing in a couple of insulated shopping bags to help keep produce cool and fresh when transporting. When shopping for fruits and vegetables, look for freshness and variety, and don't be afraid to experiment with unfamiliar items.

To stock your fridge Mediterranean-style, you'll want to keep the following items on hand:

- Cheeses (unprocessed varieties)
- Fresh fish, seafood, poultry, lean pork, and other lean meat (kinds you can and will consume right away)
- Fresh fruits
- Fresh vegetables
- Greek yogurt
- Haas avocados
- Lean cuts of fresh beef, such as brisket, flank steak, and filet mignon
- Lemons (for squeezing on fish and seafood, and for making dressings)
- Olive oil mayonnaise
- Spinach, kale, or other dark, leafy greens for salads and for adding to omelets and other dishes

What to Keep in Your Freezer

Although fresh foods are always best, it is also important to plan ahead. You don't want to end up with a hungry family (or even a hungry you) without any options. Plan to keep Mediterranean staples on hand for when you don't have time to shop or for the occasional emergency dinner. It's smart to package and freeze meats and seafood in smaller quantities so that you can pull out and thaw one or two servings at a time.

Here's what makes a well-stocked Mediterranean freezer:

- Frozen fruit
- Frozen lean meats, a variety
- Frozen poultry, whole and cut
- Frozen seafood
- Frozen vegetables

Pantry Items

An easy way to stock and organize your pantry is to think in terms of categories: produce, whole grains and baking items, proteins, and fats. If possible, arrange items so that a quick visual scan lets you know what you have on hand and what should go on your shopping list. Use nuts within a couple of months to get maximum nutrients and taste, and keep in mind that they can spoil sooner in warmer climates. Store them in airtight containers in cool, dark cupboards, or ideally in the refrigerator or freezer. Remember: If you buy canned foods, do your best to choose low-sodium and BPA-free options.

Produce

- Garlic
- Olives
- Onions
- Potatoes
- Tomatoes (a variety of crushed, diced, and whole)
- Yams

Whole grains and baking staples

- Bulgur
- Couscous
- Farro
- Flour (all-purpose and whole-wheat flour)
- Local honey
- Long-grain brown and white rice
- Oats
- Polenta
- Quinoa
- Unsweetened cereals
- Unsweetened cocoa powder
- Vanilla extract

- Whole-grain bread
- Whole-grain crackers
- Whole-grain pasta

- Whole-grain pita
- Whole-wheat tortillas
- Wild rice

Proteins

- Tuna, salmon, crab, and other canned fish
- Jerky, smoked salmon, kipper snacks, and other dried meats (the fewer additives the better)
- Almonds
- Brazil nuts
- Macadamia nuts
- Peanuts
- Pecans

- Pumpkin seeds
- Sunflower seeds
- Walnuts
- Black beans
- Chickpeas (also called garbanzo beans)
- Kidney beans
- Navy beans
- Pinto beans
- White beans

Fats

- Olive oil: This oil is neutral tasting and is best reserved for low- to medium-heat cooking, because it smokes at a lower temperature.
- Extra-virgin olive oil: With a stronger olive flavor, this oil is perfect for dressing vegetables and making your own sauces.
- Canola oil: This oil is neutral-tasting and has a higher smoking point.
- Avocado oil: Wonderful for making dressings and sauces, this mild oil has a delicious nutty flavor. It does not taste like avocados.
- Grapeseed oil: With a clean, light taste, grapeseed oil is excellent for dressings, emulsions like mayonnaise, herb infusions, and baked goods.

Your Mediterranean Spice Rack

Spices are little items that make a big difference in your cooking. Technically vegetables in concentrated form, herbs and spices contain healthful phytonutrient compounds, including antioxidants. Keep your spice rack well stocked and your food well flavored.

- Basil
- Chili powder
- Cinnamon

- Coriander
- Curry
- Garlic powder

- Italian spice blend
- Mint
- Onion powder
- Oregano
- Pepper

- Rosemary
- Sea salt
- Smoked paprika
- Thyme
- Turmeric

CHAPTER THREE

Soups

Soups are perfect recipes for slow cooking, and they also make the most of smaller cuts of meat and extra vegetables. These soups are flexible, so if you have a favorite ingredient and want to experiment within a flavor profile (see page 10), you will likely get good results.

Moroccan Lentil Soup

Vegetable Soup Provençal

Chicken and Pasta Soup

Sausage Fennel Minestrone

Mediterranean Vegetable Stew

Spanish Vegetable Stew

Kale and Cannellini Stew with Farro

Southern Italian Chicken Stew

Moroccan Seafood Stew

Mediterranean Beef Stew with Rosemary and Balsamic Vinegar

Tuscan Beef Stew

Moroccan Lentil Soup

SERVES 6

If lentils are something you don't usually eat, take this opportunity to get acquainted with them. Just one serving of this soup is packed with protein, vitamins A and C, and potassium— one of the nutrients Americans are most likely to be lacking.

1 CUP CHOPPED ONIONS

1 CUP CHOPPED CARROTS

3 CLOVES GARLIC, MINCED

1 TEASPOON EXTRA-VIRGIN OLIVE OIL

1 TEASPOON GROUND CUMIN

½ TEASPOON GROUND CORIANDER

1 TEASPOON GROUND TURMERIC

¼ TEASPOON GROUND CINNAMON

¼ TEASPOON FRESHLY GROUND BLACK PEPPER

4 CUPS VEGETABLE STOCK

1½ CUPS CHOPPED CAULIFLOWER

1 CUP DRY LENTILS

ONE 28-OUNCE CAN DICED TOMATOES, WITH THE JUICE

1 TABLESPOON TOMATO PASTE

1 CUP GENTLY PACKED CHOPPED FRESH SPINACH

¼ CUP CHOPPED FRESH CILANTRO

1 TABLESPOON RED WINE VINEGAR, PLUS MORE FOR SERVING (OPTIONAL)

1. Combine the onions, carrots, garlic, olive oil, cumin, coriander, turmeric, cinnamon, and ¼ teaspoon black pepper in the slow cooker.

2. Add the vegetable stock, cauliflower, lentils, tomatoes, and tomato paste and stir to combine.

3. Cover and cook on high for 4 to 5 hours or on low for 8 to 10 hours, until the lentils are tender.

4. During the last 30 minutes of cooking, stir in the spinach.

5. Just before serving, stir in the cilantro and vinegar. Serve hot with more vinegar, if desired.

Vegetable Soup Provençal

SERVES 8

Provençal *refers to things originating in Provence in the south of France. The herbes de Provence, as well as the wine and escarole, are what distinguish this dish as uniquely French. It is a light, flavorful soup to serve anytime.*

SOUP

2 TABLESPOONS EXTRA-VIRGIN OLIVE OIL

3 LEEKS (WHITE AND TENDER GREEN PARTS), HALVED LENGTHWISE, CLEANED, AND CUT
  CROSSWISE INTO ½-INCH HALF-MOONS

3 RIBS CELERY, COARSELY CHOPPED

3 MEDIUM CARROTS, COARSELY CHOPPED

2 TEASPOONS HERBES DE PROVENCE

½ CUP DRY WHITE WINE

ONE 15-OUNCE CAN DICED TOMATOES WITH THE JUICE

8 CUPS CHICKEN OR VEGETABLE STOCK

2 MEDIUM ZUCCHINI, CUT INTO ½-INCH CHUNKS

2 CUPS FRESH OR FROZEN, THAWED PEAS

1 HEAD ESCAROLE, CUT INTO 1-INCH PIECES

TWO 15-OUNCE CANS SMALL WHITE BEANS, DRAINED AND RINSED

PISTOU

2 CUPS FIRMLY PACKED FRESH BASIL LEAVES

6 GARLIC CLOVES, PEELED

½ CUP EXTRA-VIRGIN OLIVE OIL

SEA SALT

BLACK PEPPER

To make the soup:

1. In a large skillet, heat the olive oil over medium-high heat. Add the leeks, celery, carrots, and herbes de Provence and sauté until the carrots begin to soften, about 3 minutes.

continued ▶

Vegetable Soup Provençal *continued* ▶

2. Add the wine, and cook to allow the wine to evaporate a bit, about 2 minutes. Transfer the contents of the skillet to the slow cooker.

3. Add the tomatoes, stock, zucchini, peas, escarole, and beans to the slow cooker and stir to combine. Cover and cook on high for 2 hours or on low for 4 hours.

To make the pistou:

1. In a blender or food processor, combine the basil and garlic and pulse to break them up.

2. With the machine running, add ¼ cup of the olive oil.

3. Scrape down the sides of the blender. Season with salt and black pepper, if necessary.

4. If the pistou is very thick, add more olive oil, 1 to 2 teaspoons at a time. The pistou should hold together and not be runny.

5. Transfer the pistou to an airtight glass jar, and float the remaining olive oil on the top to prevent the basil from discoloring.

6. When ready to serve, season with salt and pepper, as necessary. Ladle the hot soup into bowls, and add 1 to 2 dollops of pistou onto the center of each serving.

Chicken and Pasta Soup

SERVES 6

Meet the Mediterranean, slow cooker version of classic chicken soup. Whether you have a bad cold or are just chasing some good memories, this recipe is a keeper. Serve with crackers, if you like.

6 BONELESS SKINLESS CHICKEN THIGHS
4 CARROTS, CUT INTO 1-INCH PIECES
4 STALKS CELERY, CUT INTO ½-INCH PIECES
1 MEDIUM YELLOW ONION, HALVED
2 GARLIC CLOVES, MINCED
2 BAY LEAVES
SEA SALT
BLACK PEPPER
6 CUPS CHICKEN STOCK
½ CUP SMALL PASTA LIKE STELLINE OR ALPHABET
¼ CUP CHOPPED FRESH FLAT-LEAF PARSLEY

1. In the slow cooker, place the chicken, carrots, celery, onion, and garlic. Add the bay leaves and season with salt and pepper.

2. Add the chicken stock. Cover and cook on high for 4 to 5 hours, or on low for 7 to 8 hours, until the chicken is cooked through and tender.

3. About 20 minutes before serving, transfer the chicken to a bowl. Let the chicken cool until it can comfortably be handled.

4. Remove and discard the onion and bay leaves. If the slow cooker is on the low setting, turn it to high.

5. Add the pasta to the slow cooker, cover, and cook until tender, 15 to 18 minutes.

6. Meanwhile, shred the chicken.

7. Stir the chicken into the soup along with the parsley. When the chicken is heated through, about 5 minutes, serve the soup hot.

Sausage Fennel Minestrone

MAKES SIX 2-CUP SERVINGS

Treat your taste buds to the delicious combination of Italian sausage and fennel in this hardy minestrone soup. Greens, pasta, beans, and vegetables make this dish a complete meal.

6 CUPS CHICKEN STOCK
2 TABLESPOONS TOMATO PASTE
1 LARGE YELLOW ONION, CHOPPED
1 CUP DICED FENNEL
½ CUP CHOPPED CELERY
1 15-OUNCE CAN CANNELLINI BEANS
1 28-OUNCE CAN DICED TOMATOES WITH THE JUICE
½ TEASPOON SEA SALT
1 BAY LEAF
½ TEASPOON DRIED THYME
1 POUND HOT ITALIAN SAUSAGE, CASINGS REMOVED
2 CUPS COOKED ORECCHIETTE PASTA
2 CUPS STEMMED, CHOPPED KALE OR SWISS CHARD

1. In the slow cooker, combine the chicken stock, tomato paste, onion, fennel, celery, cannellini, and tomatoes. Add ½ teaspoon salt and the bay leaf and thyme.

2. In a nonstick medium skillet over medium-high heat, sauté the sausage, breaking it up into small chunks, until browned, about 5 minutes. Drain on a paper towel–lined plate.

3. Add the browned sausage to the slow cooker. Cover and cook on high for 4 hours.

4. Stir in the orecchiette and kale, and cook until heated through, about 5 minutes. Serve hot.

Mediterranean Vegetable Stew

SERVES 10

This delicious vegetarian dish will delight even the most devout meat-eaters. The spices ramp up the flavor of the vegetables, and the raisins add a surprising note of sweetness.

1 BUTTERNUT SQUASH, PEELED, SEEDED, AND CUBED

2 CUPS UNPEELED CUBED EGGPLANT

2 CUPS CUBED ZUCCHINI

10 OUNCES FRESH OKRA, CUT INTO SLICES

ONE 8-OUNCE CAN TOMATO SAUCE

1 LARGE YELLOW ONION, CHOPPED

1 RIPE TOMATO, CHOPPED

1 CARROT, THINLY SLICED

½ CUP VEGETABLE STOCK

⅓ CUP RAISINS

2 CLOVES GARLIC, MINCED

½ TEASPOON GROUND CUMIN

½ TEASPOON GROUND TURMERIC

¼ TEASPOON RED PEPPER FLAKES

¼ TEASPOON GROUND CINNAMON

1 TEASPOON PAPRIKA

1. In the slow cooker, combine the butternut squash, eggplant, zucchini, okra, tomato sauce, onion, tomato, carrot, vegetable stock, raisins, and garlic. Sprinkle in the cumin, turmeric, red pepper flakes, cinnamon, and paprika.

2. Cover and cook on low for 8 to 10 hours, or until the vegetables are fork-tender. Serve hot.

Spanish Vegetable Stew

SERVES 4

The chickpeas and potatoes lend substance to this Spanish-style dish, and the wine and thyme give it extra flavor. The result—a unique mixture of flavors that is at once light on the palate yet deeply satisfying.

2 TABLESPOONS OLIVE OIL

3 SHALLOTS, CHOPPED

1 LARGE CARROT, SLICED

2 GARLIC CLOVES, MINCED

1 POUND RED POTATOES, QUARTERED

1 RED BELL PEPPER, CHOPPED

ONE 9-OUNCE PACKAGE QUARTERED ARTICHOKE HEARTS

ONE 15-OUNCE CAN DICED TOMATOES WITH THE JUICE

1½ CUPS COOKED CHICKPEAS

⅓ CUP DRY WHITE WINE

1½ CUPS VEGETABLE STOCK

1 TEASPOON MINCED FRESH THYME LEAVES (OR ½ TEASPOON DRIED)

1 TEASPOON MINCED FRESH OREGANO LEAVES (OR ½ TEASPOON DRIED)

1 LARGE BAY LEAF

SEA SALT

BLACK PEPPER

1. Heat the oil in a large skillet over medium heat. Add the shallots, carrot, and garlic, and cook, stirring often, until the vegetables are soft, about 8 minutes. Put the vegetables in the slow cooker.

2. Add the potatoes, bell pepper, artichoke hearts, tomatoes, chickpeas, wine, and stock to the slow cooker.

3. Sprinkle in the thyme, oregano, and bay leaf, and season with salt and pepper. Cover and cook on low for 6 to 8 hours. Serve hot.

Kale and Cannellini Stew with Farro

SERVES 6

Farro is a type of hulled wheat with a chewy texture and nutty flavor. Ready in just a few hours, this stew also features super-food kale and flavorful feta cheese for garnish.

4 CUPS VEGETABLE OR CHICKEN STOCK

ONE 14-OUNCE CAN DICED FIRE-ROASTED TOMATOES

1 CUP FARRO, RINSED

1 LARGE YELLOW ONION, CHOPPED

2 MEDIUM CARROTS, HALVED LENGTHWISE AND THINLY SLICED CROSSWISE

2 STALKS CELERY, COARSELY CHOPPED

4 CLOVES GARLIC, MINCED

½ TEASPOON RED PEPPER FLAKES

¼ TEASPOON SEA SALT

4 CUPS FRESH KALE, STEMMED AND COARSELY CHOPPED

ONE 15-OUNCE CAN CANNELLINI BEANS, RINSED AND DRAINED

3 TABLESPOONS FRESH LEMON JUICE

½ CUP CRUMBLED FETA CHEESE

FRESH FLAT-LEAF PARSLEY OR BASIL, CHOPPED, FOR GARNISH

1. Combine the stock, tomatoes, farro, onion, carrots, celery, and garlic in the slow cooker.

2. Add the red pepper flakes and ¼ teaspoon salt.

3. Cover and cook on high for 2 hours, or until the farro is tender yet chewy.

4. Add the kale, cannellini, and lemon juice and stir. Cover and cook 1 additional hour.

5. Serve hot, sprinkled with the feta cheese and parsley.

Southern Italian Chicken Stew

SERVES 4

This basic yet delicious stew makes a satisfying light meal. With the pasta, tender chicken, and variety of vegetables and spices, this dish provides a complete range of nutrition, not to mention the familiar, tasty flavors of Southern Italy.

2 TEASPOONS OLIVE OIL

4 SKINLESS CHICKEN BREASTS, CUT INTO 1-INCH PIECES

1 TEASPOON GARLIC POWDER

¼ TEASPOON BLACK PEPPER

½ TEASPOON SEA SALT

2 TEASPOONS DRIED OREGANO

ONE 28-OUNCE CAN DICED TOMATOES WITH THE JUICE

1 YELLOW ONION, DICED

2 CLOVES GARLIC, MINCED

ONE 8-OUNCE PACKAGE PASTA

ONE 14-OUNCE CAN ARTICHOKE HEARTS, DRAINED AND QUARTERED

ONE 6-OUNCE CAN BLACK OLIVES, DRAINED

1. Heat the olive oil in a large skillet over medium-high heat.

2. Sprinkle the chicken pieces with the garlic powder, black pepper, sea salt, and oregano.

3. Sauté the chicken for 6 to 8 minutes, turning frequently, until browned on all sides. Remove to a paper towel–lined plate to drain.

4. Place the chicken in the slow cooker. Top with the tomatoes, onion, and garlic. Cover and cook on low for 4 hours.

5. After 3 hours, add the pasta to the slow cooker. Cover and continue cooking.

6. After 4 hours, stir in the artichoke hearts and olives. Turn up the heat to high. Cover and cook for 10 minutes more, or until the artichokes and olives are heated through. Serve hot.

Moroccan Seafood Stew

SERVES 8

This soup is bound to be one of the most unique soups you have ever tasted—and one of the most delicious. This dish is a special treat, thanks to the fresh seafood and saffron.

2 TABLESPOONS EXTRA-VIRGIN OLIVE OIL

1 LARGE YELLOW ONION, FINELY CHOPPED

1 MEDIUM RED BELL PEPPER, CUT INTO ½-INCH STRIPS

1 MEDIUM YELLOW BELL PEPPER, CUT INTO ½-INCH STRIPS

4 GARLIC CLOVES, MINCED

1 TEASPOON SAFFRON THREADS, CRUSHED IN THE PALM OF YOUR HAND

1½ TEASPOONS SWEET PAPRIKA

¼ TEASPOON HOT PAPRIKA

½ TEASPOON GROUND GINGER

ONE 15-OUNCE CAN DICED TOMATOES, WITH THE JUICE

¼ CUP FRESH ORANGE JUICE

2 POUNDS SKINLESS SEA BASS FILLETS

¼ CUP FINELY CHOPPED FRESH FLAT-LEAF PARSLEY

¼ CUP FINELY CHOPPED FRESH CILANTRO

SEA SALT

BLACK PEPPER

1 NAVEL ORANGE, THINLY SLICED, FOR GARNISH

1. In a large skillet, heat the olive oil over medium-high heat. Sauté the onion, bell peppers, and garlic. Add the saffron, sweet paprika, hot paprika, and ginger. Cook for 3 minutes, or until the onion begins to soften.

2. Add the tomatoes and sauté for another 2 minutes, to blend the flavors.

3. Transfer the mixture to the slow cooker and stir in the orange juice. Place the sea bass on top of the tomato mixture, and spoon some of the mixture over the fish. Cover and cook on high for 2 hours or on low 3 to 4 hours.

continued ▶

Moroccan Seafood Stew *continued* ▶

4. At the end of the cooking time, the sea bass should be opaque in the center.

5. Using a fish spatula or any thin spatula, carefully lift the fish out of the slow cooker, transfer it to a serving platter, and cover it loosely with aluminum foil.

6. Skim off any excess fat from the sauce, stir in the parsley and cilantro, and season with salt and pepper.

7. Spoon some of the sauce over the fish, and garnish with the orange slices. Serve hot, passing the remaining sauce on the side.

Mediterranean Beef Stew with Rosemary and Balsamic Vinegar

SERVES 6

The perfect choice to warm you up on a cold winter evening, this beef stew has a rich, distinctive flavor. The balsamic vinegar, olives, rosemary, and capers accompany the beef and mushrooms perfectly.

8 OUNCES MUSHROOMS, SLICED

1 LARGE YELLOW ONION, DICED

2 TABLESPOONS OLIVE OIL

2 POUNDS CHUCK STEAK, TRIMMED AND CUT INTO BITE-SIZE PIECES

1 CUP BEEF STOCK

ONE 15-OUNCE CAN DICED TOMATOES, WITH THE JUICE

½ CUP (4 OUNCES) TOMATO SAUCE

¼ CUP BALSAMIC VINEGAR

ONE 5-OUNCE CAN CHOPPED BLACK OLIVES

½ CUP THINLY SLICED GARLIC CLOVES

2 TABLESPOONS FINELY CHOPPED FRESH ROSEMARY (OR 1 TABLESPOON
    DRIED ROSEMARY)

2 TABLESPOONS FINELY CHOPPED FRESH FLAT-LEAF PARSLEY (OR 1 TABLESPOON
    DRIED PARSLEY)

2 TABLESPOONS CAPERS, DRAINED

SEA SALT

BLACK PEPPER

1. Place the mushrooms and onion in the slow cooker.

2. Heat the olive oil in a large skillet over medium-high heat. Add the beef and cook until well browned, stirring often, for 10 to 15 minutes. Don't rush the browning step, and decrease the heat to medium if the beef browns too quickly. Add the beef to the slow cooker.

continued ▶

Mediterranean Beef Stew with Rosemary and Balsamic Vinegar *continued* ▶

3. Add the beef stock to the skillet and simmer for 5 minutes or until slightly reduced, scraping up the flavorful brown bits from the bottom of the pan with a wooden spoon. Add the stock to the slow cooker.

4. Add the diced tomatoes, tomato sauce, vinegar, olives, garlic, rosemary, parsley, and capers to the slow cooker. Season with salt and pepper. Stir gently to combine. Cover and cook on low for 6 to 8 hours. (It is possible to cook on high for 3 to 4 hours, but the lower setting yields the best results.) Season with additional salt and pepper, if desired, and serve hot.

Tuscan Beef Stew

SERVES 4 TO 6

This is comfort food, pure and simple. The burgundy wine and the seasoning as well as the vegetables add an unmistakable Mediterranean flair.

1 8-OUNCE CAN TOMATO SAUCE

1½ CUPS BEEF STOCK

¾ CUP BURGUNDY WINE (OR OTHER DRY RED WINE)

ONE 14-OUNCE CAN DICED TOMATOES WITH THE JUICE

3 LARGE CARROTS, CUT INTO 1-INCH PIECES

2 POUNDS BEEF FOR STEW, CUT INTO 1-INCH CUBES

1 TEASPOON DRIED OREGANO

½ TEASPOON DRIED ROSEMARY

½ TEASPOON GARLIC POWDER

1 TEASPOON SEA SALT

½ TEASPOON BLACK PEPPER

TWO 15-OUNCE CANS CANNELLINI BEANS, DRAINED AND RINSED

1. Combine tomato sauce, beef stock, wine, tomatoes, carrots, and beef in the slow cooker.

2. Add the oregano, rosemary, garlic powder, salt, and pepper.

3. Cover and cook on low for 8 to 9 hours or until beef is fork tender.

4. Stir in the cannellini. Increase the heat to high. Cover and cook for an additional 10 minutes or until the beans are heated through. Serve hot.

CHAPTER FOUR

Pastas, Grains, and Beans

Pastas, whole grains, and legumes are central to Mediterranean cuisine. These kinds of foods are also a natural fit with the slow cooker, because this cooking method allows them plenty of time to soak up flavor. Beans in particular benefit from slow cooking because they soften well and break down nicely, making them more easily digestible.

Pastas

Minestrone Casserole

Butternut Squash Lasagna

Greek Pasta with Chicken

Pasta with Mediterranean Beef

Grains

Moroccan Oatmeal

Quinoa Chicken Chili

Rice and Turkey Slow Cooker Bake

Mediterranean Rice and Sausage

Beans

Red Beans and Rice

Borlotti Beans with Spiced
    Polenta Dumplings

Beans with Chicken Sausage
    and Escarole

Chicken Sausage Cassoulet

Slow Cooker Vegetarian Chili

Moroccan Vegetables and Chickpeas

Minestrone Casserole

SERVES 5

This pasta dish, which riffs on the favorite soup, is a heartier version suitable for a one-dish meal. Aside from just minutes of slicing, this recipe comes together in minutes, and it is a perfect choice for a weekday meal.

3 MEDIUM CARROTS, SLICED

1 MEDIUM YELLOW ONION, CHOPPED

3 CLOVES GARLIC, MINCED

1 CUP CHICKEN OR VEGETABLE STOCK

2 TEASPOONS GRANULATED SUGAR

1 TEASPOON DRIED OREGANO

½ TEASPOON DRIED ROSEMARY

½ TEASPOON SEA SALT

¼ TEASPOON BLACK PEPPER

ONE 28-OUNCE CAN DICED TOMATOES, WITH THE JUICE

ONE 15-OUNCE CAN CHICKPEAS, DRAINED AND RINSED (SEE NOTE)

ONE 6-OUNCE CAN TOMATO PASTE

½ POUND FRESH GREEN BEANS, TRIMMED AND CUT INTO BITE-SIZE PIECES

1 CUP UNCOOKED MACARONI PASTA

2 OUNCES PARMESAN CHEESE, GRATED

1. In the slow cooker, add carrots, onion, garlic, stock, and sugar and stir to combine. Add the oregano, rosemary, salt, and pepper. Add the tomatoes, chickpeas, and tomato paste and stir to combine. Cover and cook on low for 6 to 8 hours.

2. Stir in the green beans and macaroni. Increase the heat to high. Cover and cook until the beans and the macaroni are tender, about 20 minutes.

3. Serve hot, sprinkled with the Parmesan.

NOTE: FEEL FREE TO SUBSTITUTE CANNELLINI BEANS, KIDNEY BEANS, OR GREAT NORTHERN BEANS FOR THE CHICKPEAS IF YOU PREFER.

Butternut Squash Lasagna

SERVES 4 TO 6

This healthy version of lasagna uses butternut squash and whole wheat noodles and a smaller amount of mozzarella than a traditional recipe. Although the set of seasonal flavors cues to autumn and winter, don't hesitate to substitute summer squash varieties for a different season!

1 BUTTERNUT SQUASH, HALVED LENGTHWISE AND SEEDED

1 TEASPOON OLIVE OIL

½ TEASPOON SAGE

½ TEASPOON SEA SALT

¼ TEASPOON BLACK PEPPER

ONE 15-OUNCE CONTAINER RICOTTA CHEESE

½ CUP MILK

¼ CUP GRATED PARMESAN CHEESE

NONSTICK COOKING OIL SPRAY

12 OUNCES WHOLE WHEAT LASAGNA NOODLES

4 OUNCES FRESH SPINACH LEAVES

½ CUP SHREDDED PART SKIM MOZZARELLA

1. Preheat the oven to 400°F. Line a baking sheet with parchment paper.

2. Rub the olive oil on the cut surfaces of the squash. Place the squash halves, cut-side up, on the prepared baking sheet. Roast in the oven for 45 minutes or until soft. Let cool until it can be safely handled. Scoop out the flesh and purée in a blender or food processor.

3. Add the squash purée to a medium bowl, and stir in the sage, ½ teaspoon salt, and ¼ teaspoon pepper.

4. In another medium bowl, stir together the ricotta, milk, and Parmesan, and season with salt and pepper.

continued ▶

Butternut Squash Lasagna *continued* ▶

5. Coat the inside of the slow cooker with nonstick cooking oil spray. Place a layer of the noodles at the bottom. (You will have to break them to fit. Don't worry about using little pieces to fill in holes, because it will come out just fine.) Cover with one-half of the squash mixture, spreading it evenly. Place another layer of noodles on top, then one half of the spinach, and finally one-half of the ricotta mixture. Then repeat the layers: Place a layer of noodles onto the ricotta layer, followed by the remaining half of the squash mixture, followed by another layer of noodles on top, then the rest of the spinach, then the other half of the ricotta mixture, and finally the last layer of noodles. Sprinkle the mozzarella on top.

6. Cover and cook on low for 3 to 4 hours (until the noodles are tender). Serve hot.

Greek Pasta with Chicken

SERVES 4

Serve up some Greek ambience with this evocatively seasoned dish that is light yet satisfying. The aroma coming from your slow cooker will make this entrée a "can't wait" favorite for your entire family.

1 TEASPOON OLIVE OIL

1 POUND BONELESS, SKINLESS CHICKEN BREASTS, CUT INTO 1-INCH CUBES

ONE 15-OUNCE CAN DICED TOMATOES, WITH THE JUICE

1½ CUPS TOMATO JUICE

1½ CUPS CHICKEN STOCK

2 MEDIUM CARROTS, THINLY SLICED

1 MEDIUM ONION, CUT INTO WEDGES

1 STALK CELERY, FINELY CHOPPED

1 TEASPOON OREGANO

1 TEASPOON BASIL

½ TEASPOON ROSEMARY

½ TEASPOON THYME

½ TEASPOON SEA SALT

½ TEASPOON GROUND CINNAMON

1 CUP UNCOOKED MEDIUM SHELL PASTA

1 CUP CRUMBLED FETA CHEESE

1. In a large skillet, heat the olive oil over medium-high heat. Add the chicken and cook until browned, about 5 minutes. Drain off the fat. Transfer the chicken to the slow cooker.

2. Stir in the tomatoes, tomato juice, chicken stock, carrots, onion, and celery. Sprinkle in the oregano, basil, rosemary, thyme, salt, and cinnamon.

3. Cover and cook on low for 4½ to 5½ hours or on high for 2¼ to 2¾ hours.

4. If using low heat setting, turn to high heat setting. Stir in the pasta. Cover and cook for 30 to 45 minutes more or until pasta is tender.

5. Serve hot, sprinkled with feta cheese.

Pasta with Mediterranean Beef

SERVES 6

This simple, wholesome way to serve whole-grain pasta can just as easily use pork or poultry. The basil gremolata, a traditional northern Italian condiment, adds flavor and a touch of sophistication.

BASIL GREMOLATA

2 TABLESPOONS FINELY GRATED PARMESAN CHEESE

2 TABLESPOONS COARSELY CHOPPED FRESH BASIL

2 CLOVES GARLIC, MINCED

PASTA DISH

1 TABLESPOON OLIVE OIL

1½ POUNDS LEAN BEEF, CUT INTO 1-INCH CUBES

3 MEDIUM CARROTS, CUT INTO ½-INCH SLICES

1 MEDIUM YELLOW OR RED BELL PEPPER, CUT INTO 1-INCH PIECES

1 MEDIUM YELLOW ONION, CUT INTO THIN WEDGES

3 CLOVES GARLIC, MINCED

1 TEASPOON DRIED OREGANO

½ TEASPOON DRIED ROSEMARY

½ TEASPOON SEA SALT

¼ TEASPOON BLACK PEPPER

ONE 15-OUNCE CAN DICED TOMATOES WITH THE JUICE

1 CUP BEEF STOCK

6 OUNCES UNCOOKED WHOLE-GRAIN PENNE PASTA

1 MEDIUM ZUCCHINI, HALVED LENGTHWISE AND CUT INTO ¼-INCH SLICES

To make the gremolata:

In a small bowl, stir together Parmesan, basil, and garlic. Cover and refrigerate while the pasta dish cooks.

To make the pasta dish:

1. Heat the olive oil in large skillet over medium-high heat. Add the beef, in two batches, and cook until brown. Drain off the fat.

2. Transfer the beef to the slow cooker. Add the carrots, bell pepper, onion, and garlic. Sprinkle in the oregano, rosemary, salt, and pepper.

3. Pour the tomatoes and beef stock over the mixture. Cover and cook on low for 7 to 9 hours or on high for 3½ to 4½ hours.

4. Add the penne for the last hour of the cooking time.

5. Once the pasta is al dente, if using low heat setting, turn to high heat setting. Stir in the zucchini. Cover and cook for 30 minutes more.

6. Serve hot, sprinkled with the basil gremolata.

Moroccan Oatmeal

SERVES 4

Long on flavor, this delicious breakfast treat will help keep you energized in the morning. It is also naturally sweetened by fruit, enough so to be a bona fide Mediterranean dessert.

3 CUPS WATER OR MILK, ANY KIND YOU PREFER
1 CUP STEEL-CUT OATS
½ TEASPOON SEA SALT
1 TEASPOON GROUND CINNAMON
½ CUP ANY COMBINATION OF DICED DRIED APRICOTS, DATES, FIGS, AND RAISINS
    (RAISINS CAN BE WHOLE)

1. Combine the water or milk and the oats in the slow cooker. Sprinkle in the salt and cinnamon.

2. Add the dried fruit to the mixture. Cover and cook on low heat for 3 hours. Do not open and/or stir until the cooking time has elapsed and the oats are cooked.

3. Serve hot.

Quinoa Chicken Chili

SERVES 8

This innovative twist on traditional chili is as delicious as it is unique. Quinoa is a complete protein, and is gluten-free and cholesterol-free. So along with the chicken and black beans, the dish is packed with protein. To ensure great flavor with no bitterness, always rinse quinoa in a fine mesh sieve before cooking.

1 TEASPOON OLIVE OIL

½ YELLOW ONION, MINCED

2 CLOVES GARLIC, MINCED

2 LARGE BONELESS, SKINLESS CHICKEN BREASTS, DICED

1 CUP QUINOA, RINSED

ONE 28-OUNCE CAN CRUSHED TOMATOES, WITH THE JUICE

ONE 15-OUNCE CAN DICED TOMATOES WITH GREEN CHILES, WITH THE JUICE

TWO 15-OUNCE CANS BLACK BEANS, DRAINED AND RINSED

2 POUNDS CORN KERNELS, FRESH OR FROZEN AND THAWED

1 LARGE BELL PEPPER, ANY COLOR, CHOPPED

2½ CUPS CHICKEN STOCK

1 TEASPOON GROUND CUMIN

1 TEASPOON RED PEPPER FLAKES

1 TEASPOON CHILI POWDER

½ TEASPOON SEA SALT

½ TEASPOON BLACK PEPPER

ONE 8-OUNCE CONTAINER OF PLAIN GREEK YOGURT, FOR SERVING (OPTIONAL)

½ CUP GRATED PARMESAN CHEESE, FOR SERVING (OPTIONAL)

1. Heat the olive oil over medium-high heat in a medium skillet. Add the onion and garlic and sauté for 1 minute.

2. Add the chicken to the skillet and cook until browned, about 5 minutes. Put the chicken in the slow cooker (see Note).

continued ▶

Quinoa Chicken Chili *continued* ▶

3. To the slow cooker, add the quinoa, crushed tomatoes, diced tomatoes with chiles, black beans, corn, bell pepper, and chicken stock. Sprinkle in the cumin, red pepper flakes, chili powder, ½ teaspoon salt, and ½ teaspoon pepper.

4. Cover and cook on low for 5 to 7 hours. Remove the chicken, shred it, and return it to the slow cooker. Season with more salt and pepper, if necessary. Keep warm until ready to serve.

5. For serving, garnish with Greek yogurt and/or Parmesan, if desired.

NOTE: IF YOU ARE PRESSED FOR TIME, YOU MAY SKIP THE CHICKEN BROWNING STEP. IF YOU DO, OMIT THE OLIVE OIL AND ADD THE ONION, GARLIC, AND CHICKEN TO THE SLOW COOKER WHEN YOU ADD THE QUINOA AND OTHER INGREDIENTS.

Rice and Turkey Slow Cooker Bake

SERVES 6

Wholesome ingredients and spices come together to make this slow cooker meal a healthy hit. If you like, use crumbled feta cheese for serving in place of Parmigiano-Reggiano, or even Greek yogurt. You can use fresh turkey, or if you have leftover cooked turkey, add that at the end of the cooking time instead. Remember, if you don't have fresh herbs, use half the recommended amount of dried herbs instead.

NONSTICK COOKING OIL SPRAY

1½ POUNDS GROUND TURKEY

1 TEASPOON SEA SALT

½ TEASPOON BLACK PEPPER

2 TABLESPOONS CHOPPED FRESH THYME

2 TABLESPOONS CHOPPED FRESH SAGE

2 CUPS CONVERTED BROWN RICE

2 CUPS CHICKEN STOCK (OR TURKEY STOCK IF YOU HAVE IT)

1 TABLESPOON PLUS 1 TEASPOON BALSAMIC VINEGAR

1 MEDIUM YELLOW ONION, CHOPPED

2 GARLIC CLOVES, MINCED

ONE 14-OUNCE CAN STEWED TOMATOES, WITH THE JUICE

3 MEDIUM-SIZE ZUCCHINI, SLICED THINLY

¼ CUP PITTED AND SLICED KALAMATA OLIVES

¼ CUP CHOPPED FRESH FLAT-LEAF PARSLEY

½ CUP GRATED PARMIGIANO-REGGIANO CHEESE, FOR SERVING (OPTIONAL)

1. Spray a large skillet with cooking oil spray. Place over medium-high heat. Add the ground turkey, 1 teaspoon salt, ½ teaspoon pepper, 1 tablespoon of the thyme, and 1 tablespoon of the sage. Sauté until turkey is no longer pink. Drain off the fat, and place the turkey mixture into the slow cooker.

continued ▶

Rice and Turkey Slow Cooker Bake *continued* ▶

2. Add the rice, chicken stock, and vinegar and stir to combine. Add the onion, garlic, tomatoes, zucchini, and olives and stir. Add the remaining 1 tablespoon thyme, remaining 1 tablespoon sage, and parsley. Mix well.

3. Cover and cook on low for 6 to 8 hours, or on high for 3 to 4 hours.

4. Season with additional salt and pepper if needed. Serve hot with Parmigiano-Reggiano cheese sprinkled on top, if desired.

Mediterranean Rice and Sausage

SERVES 4

This simple standby can easily be made vegetarian if you omit the sausage. Or you can replace it with seafood toward the end of the cooking time if you just want a lighter version. Other similar recipes call for commercial vegetable juices, but this Mediterranean version goes au naturel with a mixture of tomato juice, spices, wine, and sautéed vegetables.

¼ CUP OLIVE OIL, PLUS 1 TABLESPOON

1½ CUPS UNCOOKED BROWN RICE

1 LARGE YELLOW ONION, CHOPPED

2 CLOVES GARLIC, MINCED

½ GREEN BELL PEPPER, CHOPPED

¾ POUND BULK GROUND ITALIAN SAUSAGE

4 CUPS TOMATO JUICE

1 TEASPOON WORCESTERSHIRE SAUCE

½ CUP RED WINE OF YOUR CHOICE

½ TEASPOON CAYENNE PEPPER

1 TEASPOON SEA SALT

¼ TEASPOON BLACK PEPPER

1. Heat ¼ cup of the olive oil over medium-high heat in a medium skillet. Add the brown rice and brown, tossing frequently, for 2 to 3 minutes. Remove the rice to a small bowl and set aside.

2. In same skillet, heat the remaining 1 tablespoon olive oil over medium-high heat. Add the onion and garlic and sauté for 1 or 2 minutes until fragrant.

3. Add the bell pepper. Cook for 2 or 3 minutes until the bell pepper has softened. Remove the vegetables to a small bowl and set aside.

continued ▶

Mediterranean Rice and Sausage *continued* ▶

4. Add the Italian sausage to the skillet. Cook over medium-high heat until just browned, about 4 minutes. Remove from the heat.

5. In a blender or food processor, purée one-half of the vegetable mix, which should now be just cool enough to handle, until just smooth.

6. To the slow cooker, add the tomato juice, Worcestershire sauce, red wine, puréed vegetables, and cooked vegetables. Add browned rice. Add the browned Italian sausage. Sprinkle in the cayenne pepper, 1 teaspoon salt, and ¼ teaspoon pepper.

7. Cover and cook on high for 2 hours. Switch to low heat and continue cooking for 5 hours.

8. Season with additional salt and pepper, as needed. Serve hot.

Red Beans and Rice

MAKES TEN 1-CUP SERVINGS (TO BE SERVED WITH 1 CUP RICE EACH)

This classic dish of the American South is actually a French import and a great example of Mediterranean flavors. Cooked with sausage as a flavor rather than the heart of the dish, this recipe follows the Mediterranean cue of using meat as a complement rather than a central feature. Served over long-grain rice, this delicious dish makes a complete meal.

7 CUPS CHICKEN OR SEAFOOD STOCK

1 POUND DRIED RED BEANS

½ TEASPOON OLIVE OIL

¾ POUND SMOKED TURKEY SAUSAGE, CUT INTO THIN SLICES

3 CELERY STALKS, CHOPPED

1 GREEN BELL PEPPER, CHOPPED

1 RED BELL PEPPER, CHOPPED

1 SWEET ONION, CHOPPED

3 GARLIC CLOVES, MINCED

1½ TEASPOONS PAPRIKA

1 TEASPOON SEA SALT

½ TEASPOON BLACK PEPPER

1 TEASPOON GARLIC POWDER

½ TEASPOON ONION POWDER

½ TEASPOON CAYENNE PEPPER

½ TEASPOON DRIED OREGANO

½ TEASPOON DRIED THYME

HOT SAUCE (OPTIONAL)

GREEN ONIONS, FINELY CHOPPED, FOR GARNISH (OPTIONAL)

RED ONION, FINELY CHOPPED, FOR GARNISH (OPTIONAL)

1. Place the stock and red beans in the slow cooker.

2. Heat the olive oil in a medium skillet over medium-high heat. Add the sausage slices and sauté until browned, about 4 minutes. Remove from heat.

continued ▶

Red Beans and Rice *continued* ▶

3. Add the celery, green bell pepper, red bell pepper, chopped onion, minced garlic, and sausage to the slow cooker. Stir to combine. Sprinkle in the paprika, 1 teaspoon salt, ½ teaspoon black pepper, garlic powder, onion powder, cayenne pepper, oregano, and thyme (see Note). Stir.

4. Cover and cook on high for 7 hours or until the beans are tender. Season with hot sauce, if desired, and/or additional salt and pepper, if desired.

5. Serve the hot red bean mixture over hot cooked rice. Garnish with green onions and/or red onions, if desired.

NOTE: MOST CREOLE SEASONING MIXES HAVE ABOUT THE SAME CONTENTS AS THE SPICES CALLED FOR HERE, INCLUDING THE SALT. SO YOU CAN PURCHASE A PREPARED CREOLE SEASONING TO SAVE TIME.

Borlotti Beans with Spiced Polenta Dumplings

SERVES 8

This healthful recipe is packed with veggies, but still tastes a little decadent thanks to the cheese and dumplings. If you're concerned about dried beans cooking evenly in a slow cooker without stirring (since opening the lid is a no-no), soaking the beans first is a great way to ensure success. The Borlotti beans are a tasty Italian-bred cranberry bean.

BEANS

1 POUND DRY BORLOTTI BEANS

6 CUPS CHICKEN STOCK

1 MEDIUM YELLOW ONION, CHOPPED

1 MEDIUM RED BELL PEPPER, DICED

2 STALKS CELERY, SLICED

1 CUP CORN KERNELS

2 CLOVES GARLIC, MINCED

1 TABLESPOON PAPRIKA

1 TABLESPOON RED PEPPER FLAKES

1 TEASPOON DRIED ROSEMARY

1 TEASPOON DRIED THYME

2 TABLESPOONS RED WINE VINEGAR

SEA SALT

continued ▶

Borlotti Beans with Spiced Polenta Dumplings *continued* ▶

POLENTA DUMPLINGS
½ CUP ALL-PURPOSE FLOUR
½ CUP CORNMEAL
½ TEASPOON BAKING POWDER
¼ SEA SALT
2 TABLESPOONS COLD BUTTER, CUT INTO CUBES
1 FRESH *PEPERONCINO*, SEEDED AND MINCED
ZEST OF 1 LIME
½ CUP BUTTERMILK
½ CUP FRESH FLAT-LEAF PARSLEY, CHOPPED, FOR SERVING
½ CUP SLICED BLACK OLIVES, FOR SERVING

To make the beans:

1. Combine the beans, stock, onion, bell pepper, celery, corn, and garlic in the slow cooker. Sprinkle with the paprika, red pepper flakes, rosemary, and thyme.

2. Cover and cook on high for 4 hours or on low for 8 hours.

To make the dumplings:

1. At 30 minutes before the end of the cooking time, whisk together the flour, cornmeal, baking powder, and ¼ teaspoon salt in a medium bowl.

2. Add the butter and use a pastry cutter or a fork to cut the butter into the flour mixture until the mixture resembles coarse meal. Add the *peperoncino* and lime zest and toss to coat. Add the buttermilk and stir to form a dough.

3. After the beans are fully cooked, stir in the red wine vinegar and 1½ teaspoons sea salt. Using generous tablespoonfuls of dough, drop 8 dumplings on top of the stew.

4. Cover and cook on high for 1 hour.

5. Serve each portion of stew topped with a dumpling. Serve hot with parsley and olives sprinkled on top.

Beans with Chicken Sausage and Escarole

SERVES 6

This colorful dish is healthful and filled with protein and flavor. It also comes together in record time, so save this one for when you're in a hurry. Most sausage varieties you buy at the market already have Mediterranean seasonings like sage and thyme in them, so that provides a flavor boost for this dish.

12 OUNCES CHICKEN SAUSAGE, CUT INTO ¼-INCH ROUNDS

1 15-OUNCE CAN CANNELLINI BEANS, DRAINED AND RINSED

1 15-OUNCE CAN CHICKPEAS, DRAINED AND RINSED

1 28-OUNCE CAN WHOLE TOMATOES, DRAINED AND CHOPPED

1½ CUPS CHICKEN STOCK

1 BAY LEAF

1 TEASPOON DRIED THYME

¼ TEASPOON RED PEPPER FLAKES

½ TEASPOON SEA SALT

¼ TEASPOON BLACK PEPPER

1 SMALL HEAD ESCAROLE, CHOPPED

¼ CUP COARSELY GRATED PARMIGIANO-REGGIANO CHEESE

2 TABLESPOONS CHOPPED FRESH FLAT-LEAF PARSLEY

1. Combine sausage, cannellini beans, chickpeas, tomatoes, and stock in the slow cooker. Sprinkle on the bay leaf, thyme, red pepper flakes, ½ teaspoon salt, and ¼ teaspoon pepper.

2. Cover and cook on low for 4 hours.

3. Stir in the escarole and cook an additional 5 to 8 minutes, until just wilted. Stir in the Parmigiano-Reggiano and parsley. Season with additional sea salt and black pepper. Serve hot.

Chicken Sausage Cassoulet

SERVES 6

The slow cooker takes the labor out of this traditional dish from Southern France. Herbes de Provence, found in most stores, is really just a simple blend of even portions of dried basil, fennel seed, marjoram, oregano, rosemary, savory, and thyme. If you want to make your own, use about ½ teaspoon of each.

NONSTICK COOKING OIL SPRAY

1 LARGE YELLOW ONION, CHOPPED

¾ CUP BABY CARROTS, HALVED LENGTHWISE

2 TABLESPOONS GARLIC, MINCED

1¼ POUNDS CHICKEN OR TURKEY SAUSAGE, CUT INTO 2-INCH SECTIONS

TWO 8-OUNCE CANS TOMATO SAUCE

1 TABLESPOON DRIED HERBES DE PROVENCE

1 TEASPOON BLACK PEPPER

TWO 15-OUNCE CANS GREAT NORTHERN BEANS, DRAINED AND RINSED

4 SLICES BACON, COOKED AND CRUMBLED

1. Coat the inside of the slow cooker crock with cooking oil spray. Add the onion, carrots, garlic, sausage, and tomato sauce. Sprinkle with the herbes de Provence and pepper. Stir to combine.

2. Cover and cook on low for 7 to 8 hours or high for 3½ to 4 hours. Add the beans to the pot in the last hour of cooking.

3. Serve hot, with bacon sprinkled on each serving.

Slow Cooker Vegetarian Chili

SERVES 4

This simple, no-nonsense recipe is as easy as it gets. You can add meat easily; brown ground or chopped meat and add it at the beginning.

ONE 28-OUNCE CAN CHOPPED WHOLE TOMATOES, WITH THE JUICE

1 MEDIUM GREEN BELL PEPPER, CHOPPED

ONE 15-OUNCE CAN RED BEANS, DRAINED AND RINSED

ONE 15-OUNCE CAN BLACK BEANS, DRAINED AND RINSED

1 YELLOW ONION, CHOPPED

1 TABLESPOON OLIVE OIL

1 TABLESPOON ONION POWDER

1 TEASPOON GARLIC POWDER

1 TEASPOON CAYENNE PEPPER

1 TEASPOON PAPRIKA

½ TEASPOON SEA SALT

½ TEASPOON BLACK PEPPER

1 LARGE HASS AVOCADO, PITTED, PEELED, AND CHOPPED, FOR GARNISH

1. Combine the tomatoes, bell pepper, red beans, black beans, and onion in the slow cooker. Sprinkle with the onion powder, garlic powder, cayenne pepper, paprika, ½ teaspoon salt, and ½ teaspoon black pepper.

2. Cover and cook on high for 4 to 6 hours or on low for 8 hours, or until thick.

3. Season with salt and black pepper if needed. Served hot, garnished with some of the avocado.

Moroccan Vegetables and Chickpeas

SERVES 6

Aromatic Moroccan spices mix with dried fruits, chickpeas, bell peppers, and potatoes in this tasty dish. Stir in Greek yogurt at the very end to add richness. Serve with quinoa or couscous with lemon wedges to make a complete meal.

1 LARGE CARROT, CUT INTO ¼-INCH ROUNDS

2 LARGE BAKING POTATOES, PEELED AND CUBED

1 LARGE BELL PEPPER, ANY COLOR, CHOPPED

6 OUNCES GREEN BEANS, TRIMMED AND CUT INTO BITE-SIZE PIECES

1 LARGE YELLOW ONION, CHOPPED

2 GARLIC CLOVES, MINCED

1 TEASPOON PEELED, GRATED FRESH GINGER

ONE 15-OUNCE CAN DICED TOMATOES, WITH THE JUICE

3 CUPS CANNED CHICKPEAS, RINSED AND DRAINED

1¾ CUPS VEGETABLE STOCK

1 TABLESPOON GROUND CORIANDER

1 TEASPOON GROUND CUMIN

¼ TEASPOON GROUND RED PEPPER

SEA SALT

BLACK PEPPER

8 OUNCES FRESH BABY SPINACH

¼ CUP DICED DRIED APRICOTS

¼ CUP DICED DRIED FIGS

1 CUP PLAIN GREEK YOGURT

1. Put the carrot, potatoes, bell pepper, green beans, onion, garlic, and ginger in the slow cooker. Stir in the diced tomatoes, chickpeas, and vegetable stock. Sprinkle with coriander, cumin, red pepper, salt, and black pepper.

2. Cover and cook on high for 6 hours or until the vegetables are tender.

3. Add the spinach, apricots, figs, and Greek yogurt, and cook and stir until the spinach wilts, about 4 minutes. Serve hot.

CHAPTER FIVE

Vegetables

Although often considered a one-dish-meaty-meal machine, your slow cooker is just as handy for side dishes and vegetable creations. This chapter will give you just a sampling of some of the wonderful vegetable dishes you can whip up in your slow cooker. Great for busy weeknights, these are also especially fabulous options on occasions like Thanksgiving and other big special-occasion meals when your oven and stove top are tied up with other dishes. Your slow cooker can take over with a great veggie dish that you can start and forget about!

Turkish Stuffed Eggplant

Eggplant Parmigiana

Ratatouille

Greek Stuffed Peppers

Slow Cooker Caponata

Barley-Stuffed Cabbage Rolls with
   Pine Nuts and Currants

Balsamic Collard Greens

Glazed Brussels Sprouts with Pine Nuts

Balsamic Root Vegetables

Sweet Potato Gratin

Orange-Glazed Carrots

Lemon-Rosemary Beets

Root Vegetable Tagine

Zucchini Casserole

Savory Butternut Squash and Apples

Stuffed Acorn Squash

Turkish Stuffed Eggplant

SERVES 6

This dish is so beautiful when served! The slow cooker is also one of the best options for eggplant, because it gets the vegetable just tender but not mushy. This method of cooking also avoids the time-consuming eggplant sweating step.

½ CUP EXTRA-VIRGIN OLIVE OIL

3 SMALL EGGPLANTS

1 TEASPOON SEA SALT

½ TEASPOON BLACK PEPPER

1 LARGE YELLOW ONION, FINELY CHOPPED

4 GARLIC CLOVES, MINCED

ONE 15-OUNCE CAN DICED TOMATOES, WITH THE JUICE

¼ CUP FINELY CHOPPED FRESH FLAT-LEAF PARSLEY

SIX 8-INCH ROUND PITA BREADS, QUARTERED AND TOASTED

1 CUP PLAIN GREEK-STYLE YOGURT

1. Pour ¼ cup of the olive oil into the slow cooker, and generously coat the interior of the crock.

2. Cut each eggplant in half lengthwise. You can leave the stem on. Score the cut side of each half every ¼ inch, being careful not to cut through the skin.

3. Arrange the eggplant halves, skin-side down, in the slow cooker. Sprinkle with 1 teaspoon salt and ½ teaspoon pepper.

4. In a large skillet, heat the remaining ¼ cup olive oil over medium-high heat. Sauté the onion and garlic for 3 minutes, or until the onion begins to soften.

5. Add the tomatoes and parsley to the skillet. Season with salt and pepper. Sauté for another 5 minutes, until the liquid has almost evaporated.

6. Using a large spoon, spoon the tomato mixture over the eggplants, covering each half with some of the mixture.

7. Cover and cook on high for 2 hours or on low for 4 hours. When the dish is finished, the eggplant should feel very tender when you insert the tip of a sharp knife into the thickest part.

8. Uncover the slow cooker, and let the eggplant rest for 10 minutes. Then transfer the eggplant to a serving dish. If there is any juice in the bottom of the cooker, spoon it over the eggplant. Serve hot with toasted pita wedges and yogurt on the side.

Eggplant Parmigiana

SERVES 6 TO 8

Parmigiana *and any of its variations are said to originate in either the southern Italian regions of Campania and Sicily or in the northern province of Parma. It is a common food preparation in the southern region. The eggplant incarnation of this dish—the oldest version— is typically made by shallow-frying sliced eggplant and layering it with cheese and tomato sauce before ultimately baking it. But the slow cooker can replace your oven for this recipe, and it does so with delicious results.*

4 MEDIUM TO LARGE EGGPLANTS, PEELED

SEA SALT FOR SWEATING EGGPLANTS, PLUS 1 TEASPOON

2 EGGS, LIGHTLY BEATEN

⅓ CUP VEGETABLE STOCK

3 TABLESPOONS ALL-PURPOSE FLOUR

OLIVE OIL FOR FRYING (ABOUT ½ CUP)

⅓ CUP SEASONED BREAD CRUMBS

½ CUP GRATED PARMESAN CHEESE, PREFERABLY PARMIGIANO-REGGIANO

1 TABLESPOON EXTRA-VIRGIN OLIVE OIL

1 YELLOW ONION, CHOPPED

ONE 28-OUNCE CAN CRUSHED TOMATOES, WITH THE JUICE

ONE 6-OUNCE CAN TOMATO PASTE

4 TABLESPOONS CHOPPED FRESH PARSLEY

2 CLOVES GARLIC, MINCED

1 TEASPOON DRIED OREGANO

1 TEASPOON SEA SALT

¼ TEASPOON BLACK PEPPER

½ CUP WHITE WINE

16 OUNCES MOZZARELLA CHEESE, SLICED

1. To prepare the eggplant, first sweat it. Cut the eggplant into ½-inch slices. Place in a large bowl in layers, sprinkling each layer with salt. Let stand 30 minutes to drain excess moisture, and then blot dry with paper towels.

2. In a medium shallow bowl, whisk the eggs with the stock and flour until smooth. Dip the eggplant slices in the batter, letting excess drip off.

3. Heat 1 tablespoon of the olive oil for frying in a large, deep skillet. Quickly sauté the eggplant, a few slices at a time, in hot olive oil, about 2 minutes. Cook the eggplant in batches, adding more olive oil for frying to the pan as necessary. Set aside the eggplant on paper towel–lined plates.

4. Combine the seasoned bread crumbs with the Parmesan cheese in a small bowl. Set aside.

5. Heat the extra-virgin olive oil in a large skillet over medium heat. Add the onion and sauté for about 3 minutes until the onion begins to soften. Add the tomatoes, tomato paste, parsley, garlic, oregano, 1 teaspoon sea salt, ¼ teaspoon black pepper, and the white wine.

6. In the slow cooker, spread the ingredients in even layers in this order: one-fourth of the eggplant slices, one-fourth of the bread crumbs, one-fourth of the tomato mixture, and one-fourth of the mozzarella cheese. Repeat, making three more layers of the eggplant, bread crumbs, tomato mixture, and mozzarella.

7. Cover and cook on low for 4 to 5 hours, until the eggplant is very tender. Serve hot, or as a snack at room temperature (a favored Sicilian way)

Ratatouille

SERVES 6

Originating in Nice in the Provence region of France, ratatouille is a traditional stewed vegetable dish similar to Spanish samfaina, *Majorcan* tombet, *and Italian* ciambotta. *The word* ratatouille *comes from the French word* touiller, *which means to toss food. Although ratatouille is usually served as a side dish, it can certainly stand alone as a meal, especially when accompanied by pasta, rice, quinoa, couscous, or bread.*

2 LARGE YELLOW ONIONS, SLICED

1 LARGE EGGPLANT, UNPEELED, SLICED

4 SMALL ZUCCHINI, SLICED

2 GARLIC CLOVES, MINCED

2 GREEN BELL PEPPERS, CUT INTO THIN STRIPS

6 LARGE TOMATOES, CUT IN ½-INCH WEDGES

1 TEASPOON DRIED BASIL

2 TEASPOONS SEA SALT

¼ TEASPOON BLACK PEPPER

2 TABLESPOONS CHOPPED FRESH FLAT-LEAF PARSLEY

¼ CUP OLIVE OIL

1. Layer one-half of each of the vegetables in the slow cooker in the following order: onion, eggplant, zucchini, garlic, bell peppers, tomatoes. Repeat with the other one-half of the vegetables.

2. Sprinkle with the basil, salt, pepper, and parsley. Drizzle the olive oil over the top.

3. Cover and cook on low for 7 to 9 hours. Serve hot.

Greek Stuffed Peppers

SERVES 4

Attractive, colorful, and delicious? This dish answers "yes" to all three. Choose bell peppers of different colors to accentuate these qualities. Serve with warm pita bread and tzatziki sauce for a complete Greek meal.

4 LARGE BELL PEPPERS, ANY COLOR (SEE NOTE)
ONE 15-OUNCE CAN CANNELLINI BEANS, RINSED AND DRAINED
1 CUP CRUMBLED FETA CHEESE
½ CUP UNCOOKED COUSCOUS
4 GREEN ONIONS, WHITE AND GREEN PARTS SEPARATED, THINLY SLICED
1 GARLIC CLOVE, MINCED
1 TEASPOON OREGANO
COARSE SEA SALT
FRESHLY GROUND BLACK PEPPER
1 LEMON CUT INTO 4 WEDGES, FOR SERVING

1. Slice a very thin layer from the base of each bell pepper so they sit upright. Slice off the tops just below stem and discard the stem only. Chop the remaining top portions, and place in a medium bowl. With a spoon, scoop out the ribs and seeds from the peppers.

2. Add the beans, feta, couscous, white parts of the green onions, garlic, and oregano to a medium bowl. Season with salt and pepper and toss to combine.

3. Stuff the peppers with bean mixture, and place them upright in the slow cooker. Cover and cook on high for 4 hours, or until the peppers are tender and the couscous is cooked.

4. To serve, sprinkle the peppers with the green parts of the green onions and plate with 1 lemon wedge alongside each pepper.

NOTE: THIS DISH WILL COOK MORE EVENLY IF YOUR BELL PEPPERS ARE ALL ABOUT THE SAME SIZE.

Slow Cooker Caponata

SERVES 6 TO 8

This classic Sicilian eggplant dish is a kind of cooked vegetable salad. It is traditionally made from chopped, fried eggplant, but more modern versions like this one cook the eggplant in healthier ways. The standard caponata with eggplant and celery is flavored with vinegar and capers in a sweet and sour sauce. This local variation includes pine nuts and raisins, but feel free to use carrots, potatoes, and/or green bell peppers instead.

1 POUND PLUM TOMATOES, CHOPPED

1 EGGPLANT, NOT PEELED, CUT INTO ½-INCH PIECES

2 MEDIUM ZUCCHINI, CUT INTO ½-INCH PIECES

1 LARGE YELLOW ONION, FINELY CHOPPED

3 STALKS CELERY, SLICED

½ CUP CHOPPED FRESH PARSLEY

2 TABLESPOONS RED WINE VINEGAR

1 TABLESPOON BROWN SUGAR

¼ CUP RAISINS

¼ CUP (4 OUNCES) TOMATO PASTE

1 TEASPOON SEA SALT

¼ TEASPOON BLACK PEPPER

¼ CUP PINE NUTS

2 TABLESPOONS CAPERS, DRAINED

3 TABLESPOONS OIL-CURED BLACK OLIVES (OPTIONAL)

1. Combine the tomatoes, eggplant, zucchini, onion, celery, and parsley in the slow cooker. Add the vinegar, brown sugar, raisins, and tomato paste. Sprinkle with the salt and pepper.

2. Cover and cook on low for 5½ hours, or until thoroughly cooked.

3. Stir in the pine nuts and capers, and olives (if using). Serve hot.

Barley-Stuffed Cabbage Rolls with Pine Nuts and Currants

SERVES 4

This dish works just as well when you assemble it the night before you cook it, so plan ahead to save yourself time. So that you can easily roll the cabbage, you'll want to trim away (not remove) the thickest part of the center vein of the cabbage leaves. If you want to mix things up a little, feel free to add cooked meat.

1 LARGE HEAD GREEN CABBAGE, CORED

1 TABLESPOON OLIVE OIL

1 LARGE YELLOW ONION, CHOPPED

3 CUPS COOKED PEARL BARLEY

3 OUNCES FETA CHEESE, CRUMBLED

½ CUP DRIED CURRANTS

2 TABLESPOONS PINE NUTS, TOASTED

2 TABLESPOONS CHOPPED FRESH FLAT-LEAF PARSLEY

½ TEASPOON SEA SALT

½ TEASPOON BLACK PEPPER

½ CUP APPLE JUICE

1 TABLESPOON APPLE CIDER VINEGAR

ONE 15-OUNCE CAN CRUSHED TOMATOES, WITH THE JUICE

1. Steam the cabbage head in a large pot over boiling water for 8 minutes. Remove to a cutting board and let cool slightly.

2. Remove 16 leaves from the cabbage head (reserve the rest of the cabbage for another use). Cut off the raised portion of the center vein of each cabbage leaf (do not cut out the vein).

3. Heat the oil in a large nonstick lidded skillet over medium heat. Add the onion, cover, and cook 6 minutes, or until tender. Remove to a large bowl.

continued ▶

Barley-Stuffed Cabbage Rolls with Pine Nuts and Currants *continued* ▶

4. Stir the barley, feta cheese, currants, pine nuts, and parsley into the onion mixture. Season with ¼ teaspoon of the salt and ¼ teaspoon of the pepper.

5. Place cabbage leaves on a work surface. On 1 cabbage leaf, spoon about ⅓ cup of the barley mixture into the center. Fold in the edges of the leaf over the barley mixture and roll the cabbage leaf up as if you were making a burrito. Repeat for the remaining 15 cabbage leaves and filling.

6. Arrange the cabbage rolls in the slow cooker.

7. Combine the remaining ¼ teaspoon salt, ¼ teaspoon pepper, the apple juice, apple cider vinegar, and tomatoes. Pour the apple juice mixture evenly over the cabbage rolls.

8. Cover and cook on high 2 hours or on low for 6 to 8 hours. Serve hot.

Balsamic Collard Greens

SERVES 5

This recipe is perfect for collard greens, a tasty green, leafy vegetable that is full of vitamins and fiber, because the vinegar offsets the slight natural bitterness of the greens. Use mixed greens if you prefer, substituting some mustard greens, for example, in place of half of the collards.

3 BACON SLICES

1 CUP CHOPPED SWEET ONION

1 POUND FRESH COLLARD GREENS, RINSED, STEMMED, AND CHOPPED

¼ TEASPOON SEA SALT

2 GARLIC CLOVES, MINCED

1 BAY LEAF

2 CUPS VEGETABLE OR CHICKEN STOCK

3 TABLESPOONS BALSAMIC VINEGAR

1 TABLESPOON HONEY

1. Cook bacon in a medium skillet over medium heat until crisp, about 6 minutes. Remove the bacon to a paper towel–lined plate to cool. Crumble the bacon.

2. Add the onion to bacon drippings and cook for 5 minutes, or until tender.

3. Add the collard greens and cook 2 to 3 minutes or until the greens begin to wilt, stirring occasionally.

4. Place the collard greens, salt, garlic, bay leaf, and stock in the slow cooker. Cover and cook on low for 3½ to 4 hours.

5. Combine the balsamic vinegar and honey in a small bowl. Stir the vinegar mixture into the collard greens just before serving. Serve hot, sprinkled with the crumbled bacon.

Glazed Brussels Sprouts with Pine Nuts

SERVES 4 TO 6

Brussels sprouts grow on long stalks, and they ripen at different rates along the same stalk. Smaller sprouts are generally tender with a delicate flavor, but those larger than 1 inch across can be bitter and strong-smelling when you cook them, so choose accordingly if that matters to you. Always trim the stem ends and remove any discolored leaves before cooking.

BALSAMIC GLAZE

1 CUP BALSAMIC VINEGAR

¼ CUP HONEY

2 POUNDS BRUSSELS SPROUTS, TRIMMED AND HALVED

2 CUPS VEGETABLE OR CHICKEN STOCK

1 TEASPOON SEA SALT

BLACK PEPPER

2 TABLESPOONS EXTRA-VIRGIN OLIVE OIL

¼ CUP PINE NUTS, TOASTED

¼ CUP GRATED PARMESAN CHEESE

1. Mix the balsamic vinegar and honey in a small saucepan over medium-high heat. Stir constantly until the sugar has dissolved. Bring to a boil, reduce the heat to low, and simmer until the glaze is reduced by half, about 20 minutes. The glaze is finished when it will coat the back of a spoon. Set aside.

2 Combine the Brussels sprouts, stock, and ½ teaspoon salt in the slow cooker. Cover and cook on high for 2 to 3 hours, or until the Brussels sprouts are tender.

3. Drain the Brussels sprouts and transfer to a serving dish. Season with salt and pepper. Drizzle with 2 tablespoons or more of the balsamic glaze and the olive oil, then sprinkle with the pine nuts and Parmesan. Serve hot.

Balsamic Root Vegetables

SERVES 6 TO 8

Root vegetables and balsamic vinegar are a match made in heaven, and just a small amount of balsamic makes this dish. Simple yet sophisticated, this side dish is special enough for even your most formal holidays and parties.

NONSTICK COOKING OIL SPRAY

1 POUND PARSNIPS, PEELED AND CUT INTO 1½-INCH CUBES

1 POUND CARROTS, PEELED AND CUT INTO 1½-INCH PIECES

2 LARGE RED ONIONS, COARSELY CHOPPED

¾ CUP DRIED APRICOTS OR FIGS

1½ POUNDS SWEET POTATOES, PEELED AND CUT INTO 1½-INCH CUBES

1 TABLESPOON LIGHT BROWN SUGAR

3 TABLESPOONS OLIVE OIL

2 TABLESPOONS BALSAMIC VINEGAR

1 TEASPOON SEA SALT

½ TEASPOON BLACK PEPPER

⅓ CUP CHOPPED FRESH FLAT-LEAF PARSLEY

1. Coat the interior of the slow cooker crock with nonstick cooking oil spray.

2. Add the parsnips, carrots, onions, and apricots in the prepared slow cooker crock, and layer the sweet potatoes over the top.

3. Whisk together the brown sugar, olive oil, balsamic vinegar, salt, and pepper in a small bowl. Pour over vegetable mixture, but do not stir.

4. Cover and cook on high for 4 to 5 hours, or until the vegetables are tender. Toss with parsley just before serving hot.

Sweet Potato Gratin

SERVES 12

Although it is both relatively light and remarkably simple, this savory sweet potato dish tastes rich and satisfying. Healthier than its cousins made with white potatoes, this recipe retains the comfort of a traditional gratin with a Mediterranean twist.

1 TABLESPOON BUTTER, AT ROOM TEMPERATURE

1 LARGE SWEET ONION, SUCH AS VIDALIA, THINLY SLICED

2 POUNDS SWEET POTATOES, PEELED AND THINLY SLICED

1 TABLESPOON ALL-PURPOSE FLOUR

1 TEASPOON CHOPPED FRESH THYME

½ TEASPOON SEA SALT

½ TEASPOON BLACK PEPPER

2 OUNCES GRATED FRESH PARMESAN CHEESE

NONSTICK COOKING OIL SPRAY

½ CUP VEGETABLE STOCK

1. Melt the butter in a medium nonstick skillet over medium heat. Add the onion and sauté 5 minutes, or until lightly browned. Remove to a large bowl.

2. Add the sweet potatoes, flour, thyme, salt, pepper, and one-half of the grated Parmesan cheese in the large bowl. Toss gently to coat the sweet potato slices with the flour mixture.

3. Coat the slow cooker with cooking oil spray. Transfer the sweet potato mixture to the slow cooker.

4. Pour the stock over the mixture. Sprinkle with the remaining Parmesan. Cover and cook on low for 4 hours or until the potatoes are tender. Serve hot.

Orange-Glazed Carrots

SERVES 8

If locating an easy and delicious side dish that your entire family will love has been tough for you, this is a wonderful dish to try. You will be amazed by how tender and delicious these carrots are.

3 POUNDS CARROTS, PEELED AND CUT INTO ¼-INCH SLICES ON THE BIAS
1½ CUPS WATER, PLUS EXTRA HOT WATER AS NEEDED
1 TABLESPOON GRANULATED SUGAR
1 TEASPOON SEA SALT
½ CUP ORANGE MARMALADE
2 TABLESPOONS UNSALTED BUTTER, SOFTENED
1½ TEASPOONS FRESH SAGE, MINCED
BLACK PEPPER (OPTIONAL)

1. Combine the carrots, 1½ cups water, sugar, and 1 teaspoon salt in the slow cooker. Cover and cook on low until the carrots are tender, 4 to 6 hours.

2. Drain the carrots, and then return to the slow cooker. Stir in the marmalade, butter, and sage. Season with additional salt and some pepper, if needed. Serve hot. (If needed, you may keep this dish on the warm setting for 1 to 2 hours before serving. Stir in some hot water before serving if it gets too thick.)

Lemon-Rosemary Beets

SERVES 7

Lemon juice does wonders for beets; it brings out the amazing natural color in the beets while tempering and maintaining the flavor. And you'll find that rosemary is the perfect spice to complement these natural tastes. For more visual flair, use a mixture of red and gold beets.

2 POUNDS BEETS, PEELED AND CUT INTO WEDGES
2 TABLESPOONS FRESH LEMON JUICE
2 TABLESPOONS EXTRA-VIRGIN OLIVE OIL
2 TABLESPOONS HONEY
1 TABLESPOON APPLE CIDER VINEGAR
¾ TEASPOON SEA SALT
½ TEASPOON BLACK PEPPER
2 SPRIGS FRESH ROSEMARY
½ TEASPOON LEMON ZEST

1. Place the beets in the slow cooker.

2. Whisk the lemon juice, extra-virgin olive oil, honey, apple cider vinegar, salt, and pepper together in a small bowl. Pour over the beets.

3. Add the sprigs of rosemary to the slow cooker.

4. Cover and cook on low for 8 hours, or until the beets are tender.

5. Remove and discard the rosemary sprigs. Stir in the lemon zest. Serve hot.

Root Vegetable Tagine

SERVES 8

A tagine is a North African dish named for the special earthenware covered pot used for cooking it. Typically, tagines are rich stews, so they feature meat, especially lamb. This vegetarian version gets its richness from hearty root vegetables and warming spices. Like other tagines, this one includes dried fruits, part of the Moroccan flavor profile.

1 POUND PARSNIPS, PEELED AND CHOPPED INTO BITE-SIZE PIECES

1 POUND TURNIPS, PEELED AND CHOPPED INTO BITE-SIZE PIECES

2 MEDIUM YELLOW ONIONS, CHOPPED INTO BITE-SIZE PIECES

1 POUND CARROTS, PEELED AND CHOPPED INTO BITE-SIZE PIECES

6 DRIED APRICOTS, CHOPPED

6 FIGS, CHOPPED

1 TEASPOON GROUND TURMERIC

1 TEASPOON GROUND CUMIN

½ TEASPOON GROUND GINGER

½ TEASPOON GROUND CINNAMON

¼ TEASPOON CAYENNE PEPPER

1 TABLESPOON DRIED PARSLEY

1 TABLESPOON DRIED CILANTRO (OR 2 TABLESPOONS CHOPPED FRESH CILANTRO)

1¾ CUPS VEGETABLE STOCK

1. Combine the parsnips, turnips, onions, carrots, apricots, and figs in the slow cooker. Sprinkle with the turmeric, cumin, ginger, cinnamon, cayenne pepper, parsley, and cilantro.

2. Pour in the vegetable stock. Cover and cook for 9 hours on low. the vegetables will be very tender. Serve hot.

Zucchini Casserole

SERVES 4

Zucchini is the Italian word for more than one of these delicious tender summer squashes. Combined with other staple Mediterranean vegetables and cheese, this zucchini dish is warm and appealing.

1 MEDIUM RED ONION, SLICED

1 GREEN BELL PEPPER, CUT INTO THIN STRIPS

4 MEDIUM ZUCCHINI, SLICED

ONE 15-OUNCE CAN DICED TOMATOES, WITH THE JUICE

1 TEASPOON SEA SALT

½ TEASPOON BLACK PEPPER

½ TEASPOON BASIL

1 TABLESPOON EXTRA-VIRGIN OLIVE OIL

¼ CUP GRATED PARMESAN CHEESE

1. Combine the onion slices, bell pepper strips, zucchini slices, and tomatoes in the slow cooker. Sprinkle with the salt, pepper, and basil.

2. Cover and cook on low for 3 hours.

3. Drizzle the olive oil over the casserole and sprinkle with the Parmesan. Cover and cook on low for 1½ hours more. Serve hot.

Savory Butternut Squash and Apples

SERVES 10

This delicious blend of naturally savory and sweet vegetables and fruits is the perfect accoutrement to a full meal. It's also one of the simplest side dishes going!

ONE 3-POUND BUTTERNUT SQUASH, PEELED, SEEDED, AND CUBED

4 COOKING APPLES (GRANNY SMITH OR HONEYCRISP WORK WELL), PEELED, CORED, AND CHOPPED

¾ CUP DRIED CURRANTS

½ SWEET YELLOW ONION SUCH AS VIDALIA, SLICED THIN

1 TABLESPOON GROUND CINNAMON

1½ TEASPOONS GROUND NUTMEG

1. Combine the squash, apples, currants, and onion in the slow cooker. Sprinkle with the cinnamon and nutmeg.

2. Cook on high for 4 hours, or until the squash is tender and cooked through. Stir occasionally while cooking (see Note).

NOTE: WHILE STIRRING IS NOT RECOMMENDED FOR MEAT DISHES FOR SAFETY REASONS, VEGETABLES ARE NOT SUBJECT TO AS MANY CONCERNS. EACH TIME YOU LIFT THE LID, HOWEVER, HEAT ESCAPES AND MUST BUILD BACK UP, SO LIFT THE LID SPARINGLY.

Stuffed Acorn Squash

SERVES 4 AS A SIDE DISH

This recipe is very simple and features the delicious and versatile acorn squash, a fall or winter squash you can keep in a cool, dry place like your pantry for several months. Soft and slightly sweet when cooked, acorn squash goes perfectly with the honey, nuts, and dried cranberries called for in this dish.

1 ACORN SQUASH
1 TABLESPOON HONEY
1 TABLESPOON OLIVE OIL (NOT EXTRA-VIRGIN)
¼ CUP CHOPPED PECANS OR WALNUTS
¼ CUP CHOPPED DRIED CRANBERRIES
SEA SALT

1. Cut the squash in half. Remove the seeds and pulp from the middle. Cut the halves in half again so you have quarters.

2. Place the squash quarters cut-side up in the slow cooker.

3. Combine the honey, olive oil, pecans, and cranberries in a small bowl.

4. Spoon the pecan mixture into the center of each squash quarter. Season the squash with salt. Cook on low for 5 to 6 hours, or until the squash is tender. Serve hot.

CHAPTER SIX

Seafood

Worldwide, seafood is a much more common source of protein than any kind of livestock or poultry. Mediterranean cuisine is full of seafood, and it's no surprise, given that each of the cultures that cook and eat this way originate in coastal countries. Seafood is a very healthful option, and a perfect way to compromise between meat-heavy eating and going completely vegetarian.

Fish and shellfish are easily digestible, full of high-quality lean protein, and they contain a mix of essential nutrients that we can only acquire through our food. Vitamins and minerals including vitamins A and D, magnesium, phosphorus, and selenium, and omega-3 fatty acids all occur naturally in abundance in seafood. There is little doubt why so many health benefits, such as lessened risk for heart disease and stroke, have been formally linked to consumption of seafood.

Mediterranean Cod au Gratin

Moroccan Sea Bass

Garlic Tilapia

Citrus Swordfish

Simple Poached Turbot

Mahi Mahi with Pineapple-Mango-
Strawberry Salsa and Lentils

Salmon with Lime Butter

Lemon-Dijon Salmon with Dill Barley

Honeyed Salmon

Cajun Shrimp

Shrimp and Artichoke Barley Risotto

Creole Crayfish

Shrimp with Marinara Sauce

Spicy Barbecued Scallops and Shrimp

Scallop and Crab Cioppino

Spicy Tomato Basil Mussels

Mediterranean Cod au Gratin

SERVES 6

This dish takes an American comfort food favorite and gives it a bit of Mediterranean flair. Pacific cod is a lean, firm, white fish with a mild flavor. If you can't find Pacific cod, try halibut or Alaskan pollock.

6 TABLESPOONS OLIVE OIL

3 TABLESPOONS ALL-PURPOSE FLOUR

1½ TEASPOONS SEA SALT

½ TABLESPOON DRY MUSTARD

1 TEASPOON ROSEMARY

¼ TABLESPOON GROUND NUTMEG

1¼ CUPS MILK

2 TEASPOONS LEMON JUICE

⅓ CUP GRATED PARMESAN CHEESE

⅓ CUP GRATED ASIAGO CHEESE

⅓ CUP GRATED ROMANO CHEESE

3 POUNDS PACIFIC COD FILLETS

1. Heat the olive oil in a small saucepan over medium heat. Stir in the flour, salt, mustard, rosemary, and nutmeg.

2. Gradually add the milk, stirring constantly until thickened.

3. Add the lemon juice, and the Parmesan, Asiago, and Romano cheeses to the saucepan. Stir until the cheeses are melted.

4. Place the fish into the slow cooker, and spoon the cheese sauce over the fish. Cover and cook on high for 1 to 1½ hours or until the fish flakes. Serve hot.

Moroccan Sea Bass

SERVES 8

Fresh, rich flavors and a mild yet hearty fish make this a delicious recipe. If you cannot get fresh sea bass, substitute halibut or snapper. You may omit the saffron if it is too expensive or inaccessible where you are, although it is a tasty, decadent treat.

2 TABLESPOONS EXTRA-VIRGIN OLIVE OIL

1 LARGE YELLOW ONION, FINELY CHOPPED

1 MEDIUM RED BELL PEPPER, CUT INTO ½-INCH STRIPS

1 MEDIUM YELLOW BELL PEPPER, CUT INTO ½-INCH STRIPS

4 GARLIC CLOVES, MINCED

1 TEASPOON SAFFRON THREADS, CRUSHED IN THE PALM OF YOUR HAND

1½ TEASPOONS SWEET PAPRIKA

¼ TEASPOON HOT PAPRIKA OR ¼ TEASPOON SMOKED PAPRIKA (OR *PIMENTÓN*)

½ TEASPOON GROUND GINGER

ONE 15-OUNCE CAN DICED TOMATOES, WITH THE JUICE

¼ CUP FRESH ORANGE JUICE

2 POUNDS FRESH SEA BASS FILLETS

¼ CUP FINELY CHOPPED FRESH FLAT-LEAF PARSLEY

¼ CUP FINELY CHOPPED FRESH CILANTRO

SEA SALT

BLACK PEPPER

1 NAVEL ORANGE, THINLY SLICED, FOR GARNISH

1. In a large skillet, heat the olive oil over medium-high heat. Add the onion, red and yellow bell peppers, garlic, saffron, sweet paprika, hot or smoked paprika, and ginger and cook, stirring often, for 3 minutes, or until the onion begins to soften.

2. Add the tomatoes and stir for another 2 minutes, to blend the flavors.

3. Transfer the mixture to the slow cooker and stir in the orange juice.

continued ▶

Moroccan Sea Bass *continued* ▶

4. Place the sea bass fillets on top of the tomato mixture, and spoon some of the mixture over the fish. Cover and cook on high for 2 hours, or on low for 3 to 4 hours. At the end of the cooking time, the sea bass should be opaque in the center.

5. Carefully lift the fish out of the slow cooker with a spatula and transfer to a serving platter. Cover loosely with aluminum foil.

6. Skim off any excess fat from the sauce, stir in the parsley and cilantro, and season with salt and pepper.

7. Spoon some of the sauce over the fish, and garnish with the orange slices. Serve hot, passing the remaining sauce on the side.

Garlic Tilapia

SERVES 3 OR 4

This recipe is so simple, you might think you're doing it wrong. But don't worry—that's it! As is sometimes the case in French and Italian cooking, a small amount of butter is used to lend texture.

2 TABLESPOONS BUTTER, AT ROOM TEMPERATURE
2 CLOVES GARLIC, MINCED
2 TEASPOONS MINCED FRESH FLAT-LEAF PARSLEY
4 TILAPIA FILLETS
SEA SALT
BLACK PEPPER

1. In a small bowl, mix the butter, garlic, and parsley to combine.

2. Pull out a large sheet of aluminum foil and put it on the counter. Place the fillets in the middle of the foil.

3. Season the fish generously with salt and pepper.

4. Evenly divide the butter mixture among the fillets and place on top.

5. Wrap the foil around the fish, sealing all sides and crimping the edges to make a packet. Place in the slow cooker, cover, and cook on high for 2 hours. Serve hot.

Citrus Swordfish

SERVES 2

Perfect when you want something light, but still satisfying, this recipe features mild, meaty grilled swordfish, enhanced with a quick ginger citrus marinade.

NONSTICK COOKING OIL SPRAY
1½ POUNDS SWORDFISH FILLETS
SEA SALT
BLACK PEPPER
1 YELLOW ONION, CHOPPED
5 TABLESPOONS CHOPPED FRESH FLAT-LEAF PARSLEY
1 TABLESPOON OLIVE OIL
2 TEASPOONS LEMON ZEST
2 TEASPOONS ORANGE ZEST
ORANGE AND LEMON SLICES, FOR GARNISH
FRESH PARSLEY SPRIGS, FOR GARNISH

1. Coat the interior of the slow cooker crock with nonstick cooking oil spray.

2. Season the fish fillets with salt and pepper. Place the fish in the slow cooker.

3. Distribute the onion, parsley, olive oil, lemon zest, and orange zest over fish.

4. Cover and cook on low for 1½ hours.

5. Serve hot, garnished with orange and lemon slices and sprigs of fresh parsley.

Simple Poached Turbot

SERVES 4

Poaching turbot (or really any fish) in the slow cooker is a snap. Turbot is a firm, white-fleshed fish perfect for poaching, and although it isn't a traditional dish for long, slow cooking, it cooks up very well in the low, even temperatures of the slow cooker. Poached turbot makes for a light meal, since it needs no oil to cook. Serve it with rice and vegetables or a salad.

1 CUP VEGETABLE OR CHICKEN STOCK
½ CUP DRY WHITE WINE
1 YELLOW ONION, SLICED
1 LEMON, SLICED
4 SPRIGS FRESH DILL
½ TEASPOON SEA SALT
FOUR 6-OUNCE TURBOT FILLETS

1. Combine the stock and wine in the slow cooker. Cover and heat on high for 20 to 30 minutes.

2. Add the onion, lemon, dill, salt, and turbot to the slow cooker. Cover and cook on high for about 20 minutes, until the turbot is opaque and cooked through according to taste. Serve hot.

Mahi Mahi with Pineapple-Mango-Strawberry Salsa and Lentils

SERVES 6

You will love the fresh, fruity salsa in this recipe, which gives you delicious, moist mahi mahi every time. Aim to purchase fillets that are about the same thickness so they will cook evenly.

1¼ CUPS VEGETABLE OR CHICKEN STOCK

1 CUP ORANGE JUICE

¾ CUP ORANGE LENTILS

½ CUP FINELY DICED CARROT

¼ CUP FINELY DICED RED ONION

¼ CUP FINELY DICED CELERY

1 TABLESPOON HONEY

SIX 4- TO-5-OUNCE MAHI MAHI FILLETS

SEA SALT

BLACK PEPPER

1 TEASPOON LEMON JUICE

SALSA

¾ CUP FINELY DICED PINEAPPLE

¾ CUP FINELY DICED MANGO

½ CUP FINELY DICED STRAWBERRIES

¼ CUP FINELY DICED RED ONION

2 TABLESPOONS CHOPPED FRESH MINT (OR 2 TEASPOONS DRIED)

2 TABLESPOONS ORANGE JUICE

1 TABLESPOON LIME JUICE

¼ TEASPOON SALT

1. Combine the stock, orange juice, lentils, carrot, onion, celery, and honey in the slow cooker.

2. Cover and cook on low for 5 to 5½ hours, or until the lentils are tender.

3. Place 1 sheet of parchment paper over the lentils in the slow cooker. Season mahi mahi lightly with salt and black pepper and place it on the parchment (skin-side down, if you have not removed the skin). Replace the lid and continue to cook on low for 25 minutes or until the mahi mahi is opaque in the center. Remove the fish by lifting out the parchment paper and putting it on a plate.

4. Stir the lemon juice into the lentils and season with salt and pepper.

To make the salsa:

1. While the fish is cooking, combine the pineapple, mango, strawberries, red onion, mint, orange juice, lime juice, and salt into a big jar. Combine and chill to give the flavors a chance to blend.

2. To serve, place about ½ cup of hot lentils on a plate and top with a mahi mahi fillet and ⅓ cup of salsa.

Salmon with Lime Butter

SERVES 2

This recipe allows you to use the slow cooker to its greatest advantage, infusing the salmon with citrus flavor slowly, resulting in a fresh, delicious, and light fish dish. Served with rice, quinoa, or other whole grain, this dish is a simple winner.

TWO 6-OUNCE SALMON FILLETS
1 TABLESPOON OLIVE OIL
½ TABLESPOON LIME JUICE
2 CLOVES GARLIC, MINCED
1 TEASPOON FINELY CHOPPED FRESH PARSLEY
¼ TEASPOON BLACK PEPPER

1. Spread a length of foil onto the countertop, and put the salmon fillets directly in the middle.

2. In a small bowl, combine the olive oil, lime juice, garlic, parsley, and black pepper. Brush the mixture over the fillets. Fold the foil over and crimp the sides to make a packet.

3. Place the packet into the slow cooker. Cover and cook on high for 2 hours.

4. Salmon is finished when it flakes easily with a fork. Serve hot.

Lemon-Dijon Salmon with Dill Barley

SERVES 6

The lemon-Dijon flavor is a classic for fish. It originates in the Mediterranean cuisine of Southern France. Fresh dill livens up the healthful barley, and you end up with a hearty yet light-tasting meal.

1 MEDIUM YELLOW ONION, DICED

2 TEASPOONS GARLIC, MINCED

2 TEASPOONS OLIVE OIL

2 CUPS VEGETABLE OR CHICKEN STOCK

1 CUP QUICK-COOKING BARLEY

1 TABLESPOON MINCED FRESH DILL WEED

1½ POUNDS SALMON FILLETS

SEA SALT

BLACK PEPPER

LEMON-DIJON SAUCE

⅓ CUP DIJON MUSTARD

3 TABLESPOONS OLIVE OIL

3 TABLESPOONS FRESH LEMON JUICE

⅓ CUP PLAIN GREEK YOGURT

1 CLOVE GARLIC, MINCED

1. Combine the onion, garlic, and oil in a microwave-safe bowl. Heat in the microwave on 70 percent power for 4 to 5 minutes, stirring occasionally. Put into the slow cooker.

2. Add the stock, barley, and dill weed to the slow cooker and stir.

continued ▶

Lemon-Dijon Salmon with Dill Barley *continued* ▶

3. Season the salmon fillets with salt and pepper, and gently place them on top of the barley mixture.

4. Cover and cook on low for about 2 hours, until the salmon and barley are cooked through.

To make the lemon-dijon sauce:

1. In a small bowl, whisk together the Dijon mustard, olive oil, lemon juice, Greek yogurt, and garlic. Set aside and allow the flavors to blend.

2. To serve, place some barley on a plate and top with a salmon fillet. Spoon the lemon-Dijon sauce over the top of the salmon.

Honeyed Salmon

SERVES 6

It doesn't get much easier than this dish—and it's just as delicious as it is easy! Serve it with pasta, rice, quinoa, couscous, or any other healthful starch to make this a satisfying meal.

SIX 6-OUNCE SALMON FILLETS
½ CUP HONEY
2 TABLESPOONS LIME JUICE
3 TABLESPOONS WORCESTERSHIRE SAUCE
1 TABLESPOON WATER
2 CLOVES GARLIC, MINCED
1 TEASPOON GROUND GINGER
½ TEASPOON BLACK PEPPER

1. Place the salmon fillets in the slow cooker.

2. In medium bowl, whisk the honey, lime juice, Worcestershire sauce, water, garlic, ginger, and pepper. Pour sauce over salmon.

3. Cover and cook on high for 1 hour.

Cajun Shrimp

SERVES 6

Although Cajun cuisine is technically an American style of cooking, named for the French-speaking Acadian or "Cajun" immigrants of Louisiana, it is characteristic of its parent cuisine, which is from the south of France. Bell peppers, onions, and celery are aromatic vegetables central to Cajun and Creole cuisines, and they tend to be roughly chopped in most recipes as in the French mirepoix, which adds carrot.

¾ POUND ANDOUILLE SAUSAGE, CUT INTO ½-INCH ROUNDS (YOU MAY SUBSTITUTE KIEL-
    BASA IF YOU CANNOT FIND ANDOUILLE SAUSAGE)

1 RED ONION, SLICED INTO WEDGES

2 GARLIC CLOVES, MINCED

2 CELERY STALKS, COARSELY CHOPPED

1 RED OR GREEN BELL PEPPER, COARSELY CHOPPED

2 TABLESPOONS ALL-PURPOSE FLOUR

1 28-OUNCE CAN DICED TOMATOES, WITH THEIR JUICE

¼ TEASPOON CAYENNE PEPPER

COARSE SEA SALT

½ POUND LARGE SHRIMP, PEELED AND DEVEINED

2 CUPS FRESH OKRA, SLICED (YOU MAY SUBSTITUTE FROZEN AND THAWED,
    IF NECESSARY)

1. Put the sausage, onion, garlic, celery, and bell pepper into the slow cooker. Sprinkle with the flour and toss to coat.

2. Add the tomatoes and ½ cup water. Sprinkle with the cayenne pepper and season with salt.

3. Cover and cook on high for 3½ hours or on low for 7 hours, until the vegetables are tender.

4. Add the shrimp and okra. Cover and cook until the shrimp are opaque throughout, on high for 30 minutes or on low for 1 hour. Serve hot.

Shrimp and Artichoke Barley Risotto

SERVES 4

Risotto is an Italian rice dish. To make it, the rice is carefully cooked in stock until it reaches a creamy consistency. Risotto, one of the most common ways to serve rice in Italy, requires a lot of attention to ensure that it doesn't burn. The slow cooker makes this part so much easier!

3 CUPS SEAFOOD STOCK (OR CHICKEN STOCK)
1 TEASPOON OLIVE OIL
1 YELLOW ONION, CHOPPED
3 CLOVES GARLIC, MINCED
ONE 9-OUNCE PACKAGE FROZEN ARTICHOKE HEARTS, THAWED AND QUARTERED
1 CUP UNCOOKED PEARL BARLEY
BLACK PEPPER
1 POUND SHRIMP, PEELED AND DEVEINED
2 OUNCES PARMESAN OR PECORINO ROMANO CHEESE, GRATED
2 TEASPOONS LEMON ZEST
4 OUNCES FRESH BABY SPINACH

1. Bring the stock to a boil in a medium saucepan. Remove from the heat and set aside.

2. In a nonstick medium skillet over medium-high heat, heat the olive oil. Add the onion and sauté until tender, about 5 minutes. Add the garlic and sauté for 1 more minute.

3. Transfer the onion and garlic to the slow cooker and add the artichoke hearts and barley. Season with some pepper. Stir in the seafood stock.

4. Cover and cook on high for 3 hours, or until the barley is tender and the liquid is just about all absorbed.

5. About 15 minutes before the cooking time is completed, stir in the shrimp and grated cheese. Cover and continue to cook on high for another 10 minutes, or until the shrimp are opaque.

6. Add the lemon zest and fold in the baby spinach, stirring until it's wilted, about 1 minute.

7. Divide the risotto among the serving bowls and serve hot.

Creole Crayfish

SERVES 2

Crayfish are common in the Mediterranean countries of Europe and are most popular in French cuisine. You may substitute other seafood if you like. If you do, use precooked crab or lobster meat, and uncooked shrimp or scallops. This recipe is simple to prepare and easy to cook in the slow cooker. Serve it over hot cooked rice or pasta for a complete meal.

1½ CUPS DICED CELERY

1 LARGE YELLOW ONION, CHOPPED

2 SMALL BELL PEPPERS, ANY COLORS, CHOPPED

1 8-OUNCE CAN TOMATO SAUCE

1 28-OUNCE CAN WHOLE TOMATOES, BROKEN UP, WITH THE JUICE

1 CLOVE GARLIC, MINCED

1 TEASPOON SEA SALT

¼ TEASPOON BLACK PEPPER

6 DROPS HOT PEPPER SAUCE (LIKE TABASCO)

1 POUND PRECOOKED CRAYFISH MEAT

1. Place the celery, onion, and bell peppers in the slow cooker. Add the tomato sauce, tomatoes, and garlic. Sprinkle with the salt and pepper and add the hot sauce.

2. Cover and cook on high for 3 to 4 hours or on low for 6 to 8 hours.

3. About 30 minutes before the cooking time is completed, add the crayfish.

4. Serve hot.

Shrimp with Marinara Sauce

SERVES 4

Marinara sauce actually means mariner's sauce. It is most common in the coastal regions of Italy. Made with tomatoes, garlic, and herbs, it can be varied by adding capers, olives, red wine, and spices. Just about everyone likes marinara sauce.

ONE 15-OUNCE CAN DICED TOMATOES, WITH THE JUICE

ONE 6-OUNCE CAN TOMATO PASTE

1 CLOVE GARLIC, MINCED

2 TABLESPOONS MINCED FRESH FLAT-LEAF PARSLEY

½ TEASPOON DRIED BASIL

1 TEASPOON DRIED OREGANO

1 TEASPOON GARLIC POWDER

1½ TEASPOONS SEA SALT

¼ TEASPOON BLACK PEPPER

1 POUND COOKED SHRIMP, PEELED AND DEVEINED

2 CUPS HOT COOKED SPAGHETTI OR LINGUINE, FOR SERVING

½ CUP GRATED PARMESAN CHEESE, FOR SERVING

1. Combine the tomatoes, tomato paste, and minced garlic in the slow cooker. Sprinkle with the parsley, basil, oregano, garlic powder, salt, and pepper.

2. Cover and cook on low for 6 to 7 hours.

3. Turn up the heat to high, stir in the cooked shrimp, and cover and cook on high for about 15 minutes longer.

4. Serve hot over the cooked pasta. Top with Parmesan cheese.

Spicy Barbecued Scallops and Shrimp

SERVES 2

The word barbecue *derives from the Spanish* barbacoa, *which came to mean meats smoked and cooked over wood at low temperatures. Spanish explorers found Caribbean islanders cooking meats in this way and brought the method home. It became popular mostly in coastal areas of Spain and France, was eventually imported to America, and is the barbecue most of us think of today.*

½ TEASPOON PAPRIKA

½ TEASPOON GARLIC POWDER

¼ TEASPOON ONION POWDER

¼ TEASPOON CAYENNE PEPPER

¼ TEASPOON DRIED OREGANO

¼ TEASPOON DRIED THYME

½ TEASPOON SEA SALT

½ TEASPOON BLACK PEPPER

2 CLOVES GARLIC, MINCED

½ CUP OLIVE OIL

¼ CUP WORCESTERSHIRE SAUCE

1 TABLESPOON HOT PEPPER SAUCE (LIKE TABASCO)

JUICE OF 1 LEMON

1 POUND SCALLOPS

1 POUND LARGE SHRIMP, UNPEELED

1 GREEN ONION, FINELY CHOPPED

1. Combine the paprika, garlic powder, onion powder, cayenne pepper, oregano, thyme, ½ teaspoon salt, and ¼ teaspoon black pepper.

2. Combine the paprika blend, garlic, olive oil, Worcestershire sauce, hot pepper sauce, and lemon juice in the slow cooker. Season with salt and pepper.

3. Cover and cook on high for 30 minutes or until hot.

4. Rinse the scallops and shrimp, and drain.

5. Spoon one-half of the sauce from the slow cooker into a glass measuring cup.

6. Place the scallops and shrimp in the slow cooker with the remaining sauce. Drizzle with the sauce in the measuring cup, and stir to coat.

7. Cover and cook on high for 30 minutes, until the scallops and shrimp are opaque.

8. Turn the heat to warm for serving. Sprinkle with the chopped green onion to serve.

Scallop and Crab Cioppino

SERVES 4

Cioppino is a thick fish stew that was invented in San Francisco in the twentieth century. But it is considered an Italian-American dish and is similar to various Mediterranean fish soups and stews from Italy as well as French bouillabaisse and Spanish suquet de peix from Catalonia. Typically, cioppino is made from whatever seafood is fresh, so feel free to substitute other fresh shellfish or fish you can find locally. Options include clams, Dungeness crab, fish, mussels, shrimp, and squid. Serve this dish with a toasted baguette.

COOKING OIL SPRAY

1 MEDIUM YELLOW ONION, FINELY CHOPPED

4 CLOVES GARLIC, MINCED

ONE 15-OUNCE CAN DICED TOMATOES, WITH THE JUICE

ONE 10-OUNCE CAN DICED TOMATOES WITH GREEN CHILES

2 CUPS SEAFOOD STOCK

1 CUP RED WINE

3 TABLESPOONS CHOPPED FRESH BASIL

2 BAY LEAVES

1 POUND COOKED CRABMEAT, SHREDDED

1½ POUNDS SCALLOPS

SEA SALT

BLACK PEPPER

¼ CUP FRESH FLAT-LEAF PARSLEY, FOR GARNISH

1. Coat a large sauté pan with cooking oil spray and heat over medium-high heat. Add the onion and sauté for about 5 minutes, until softened.

2. Add the garlic and sauté until golden and fragrant, about 2 minutes.

3. Transfer the onion and garlic to the slow cooker, and add the tomatoes, tomatoes with green chiles, stock, wine, basil, and bay leaves. Cover and cook on low for 6 hours.

4. About 30 minutes before the cooking time is completed, add the crabmeat and scallops. Cover and cook on high for 30 minutes. The seafood will turn opaque. Season to taste with salt and pepper. Serve hot, garnished with parsley.

Spicy Tomato Basil Mussels

SERVES 4

It's easy to forget that mussels are a great option when you're cooking Mediterranean cuisine, but don't, especially when using your slow cooker! They are very high in protein and B complex vitamins, and are particularly well-suited for the slow-cooker. Remember, mussels that open before cooking have gone bad, so discard those. The recipe allows for this so don't worry.

3 TABLESPOONS OLIVE OIL

4 CLOVES GARLIC, MINCED

3 SHALLOT CLOVES, MINCED

8 OUNCES MUSHROOMS, DICED

ONE 28-OUNCE CAN DICED TOMATOES, WITH THE JUICE

¾ CUP WHITE WINE

2 TABLESPOONS DRIED OREGANO

½ TABLESPOON DRIED BASIL

½ TEASPOON BLACK PEPPER

1 TEASPOON PAPRIKA

¼ TEASPOON RED PEPPER FLAKES

3 POUNDS MUSSELS

1. In a large sauté pan, heat the olive oil over medium-high heat. Cook the garlic, shallots, and mushrooms for 2 to 3 minutes, until the garlic is just a bit brown and fragrant. Scrape the entire contents of the pan into the slow cooker.

2. Add the tomatoes and white wine to the slow cooker. Sprinkle with the oregano, basil, black pepper, paprika, and red pepper flakes.

3. Cover and cook on low for 4 to 5 hours, or on high for 2 to 3 hours. The mixture is done cooking when mushrooms are fork tender.

4. Clean and debeard the mussels. Discard any open mussels.

5. Increase the heat on the slow cooker to high once the mushroom mixture is done. Add the cleaned mussels to the slow cooker and secure the lid tightly. Cook for 30 more minutes.

6. To serve, ladle the mussels into bowls with plenty of broth. Discard any mussels that didn't open up during cooking. Serve hot, with crusty bread for sopping up the sauce.

CHAPTER SEVEN

Poultry

Poultry is such an easy solution when you're looking for a quick, easy, lean protein. It also lends itself well to Mediterranean cooking, since it is so versatile and goes well with so many flavor profiles. Don't be afraid to improvise with poultry in your slow cooker. Your only real concern is to ensure that you cook the poultry thoroughly.

Chicken Mushroom Farro Risotto

SERVES 4

Farro is a whole-grain substitute for rice in this risotto, and it adds not only a chewier texture, but significantly more protein. Risotto traditionally uses special varieties of rice such as arborio to achieve the creamy texture you want from the dish, so you can't substitute just any grain into risotto. But farro does the trick beautifully, especially in a slow cooker, where it has lots of time to reach the right consistency.

2¼ CUPS CHICKEN STOCK

1 CUP WHOLE FARRO

1 POUND CREMINI OR BUTTON MUSHROOMS, HALVED, OR QUARTERED IF LARGE

2 LEEKS, WHITE AND LIGHT GREEN PARTS ONLY, HALVED, SLICED, AND RINSED

1 BAY LEAF

¼ TEASPOON GROUND NUTMEG

1¼ TEASPOONS SEA SALT

¼ TEASPOON BLACK PEPPER

4 SMALL BONELESS, SKINLESS CHICKEN THIGHS (ABOUT 1 POUND)

ONE 3-INCH PIECE PARMESAN CHEESE RIND

⅓ CUP GRATED PARMESAN, PLUS MORE FOR SERVING (OPTIONAL)

2 TABLESPOONS UNSALTED BUTTER, CUT INTO PIECES, FOR SERVING (OPTIONAL)

¼ CUP CHOPPED FRESH FLAT-LEAF PARSLEY, FOR SERVING (OPTIONAL)

1. Combine the stock, farro, mushrooms, leeks, and Parmesan rind in the slow cooker. Add the bay leaf and nutmeg, 1¼ teaspoons salt, and ¼ teaspoon pepper.

2. Arrange the chicken atop the other contents in the slow cooker. Cover and cook until the chicken is tender, on low for 6 to 7 hours or on high for 4 to 5 hours.

3. To serve, discard the Parmesan rind and bay leaf. Shred the chicken into large pieces and return to the risotto. Stir in the grated Parmesan cheese. Stir in the butter, if using.

4. Sprinkle the risotto with the parsley, if desired, and serve hot with additional grated Parmesan, if desired.

Braised Basque Chicken

SERVES 6

Basque Country is a region that encompasses the western end of the Pyrénées on the coast of the Bay of Biscay. It covers parts of southwestern France and north-central Spain. According to Food & Wine *magazine, statistics show that the Basques spend more than twice as much of their disposable income on food as we do in the United States: In other words, food is serious business. This dish, featuring colorful bell peppers and the rich tone of Serrano ham, is inspired by the cuisine from this region. The olives in the dish are technically for garnish, but don't skip them!*

3 POUNDS SKINLESS BONE-IN CHICKEN PIECES

2 TEASPOONS SEA SALT

1 TEASPOON BLACK PEPPER

4 TABLESPOONS EXTRA-VIRGIN OLIVE OIL

¼ POUND SERRANO HAM, CUT INTO ½-INCH CUBES

2 LARGE ONIONS, THINLY SLICED

2 GARLIC CLOVES, MINCED

2 MEDIUM RED BELL PEPPERS, CUT INTO ½-INCH STRIPS

2 MEDIUM YELLOW BELL PEPPERS, CUT INTO ½-INCH STRIPS

ONE 28-OUNCE CAN CHOPPED TOMATOES, WITH THE JUICE

½ CUP PITTED PICHOLINE OR OTHER GREEN OLIVES, FOR GARNISH

½ CUP PITTED NIÇOISE OLIVES, FOR GARNISH

¼ CUP FINELY CHOPPED FRESH FLAT-LEAF PARSLEY, FOR GARNISH

1. Sprinkle the chicken with 1 teaspoon of the salt and ½ teaspoon of the pepper.

2. In a large skillet, heat 2 tablespoons of the olive oil over medium-high heat. Brown the chicken on all sides, a few pieces at a time, being careful not to crowd the pan. Add an additional 1 tablespoon olive oil when needed. Transfer the browned chicken to the slow cooker.

3. Add the remaining 1 tablespoon olive oil to the skillet and sauté the ham, letting it brown a bit. Transfer to the slow cooker.

continued ▶

Braised Basque Chicken *continued* ▶

4. Add the onions, garlic, and red and yellow bell peppers to the skillet, and season with the remaining 1 teaspoon salt and ½ teaspoon pepper. Cook until the onions begin to soften, about 3 minutes.

5. Add the tomatoes to the skillet and bring to a boil, scraping up any flavorful browned bits on the bottom of the pan. Transfer the contents of the skillet to the slow cooker, covering the chicken with the mixture.

6. Cover the slow cooker and cook on high for 3 hours, or on low for 5 to 6 hours, until the chicken is cooked through.

7. Skim off any excess fat on the sauce, and season with salt or black pepper.

8. Serve the chicken hot garnished with the olives and parsley.

Spinach and Feta-Stuffed Chicken Breasts with Lemon-Dill Sauce

SERVES 6

This delicious dish takes a bit more time than some slow cooker recipes, but the results are well worth it. Rich and decadent, this recipe can be made with less fat by using milk rather than cream if you like, but you also can use just a small amount of sauce with each serving. Save time by making the lemon-dill sauce in advance and heating it again slowly over gentle heat before serving.

STUFFED CHICKEN

4 TABLESPOONS OLIVE OIL

2 TABLESPOONS FINELY CHOPPED SHALLOT

1 GARLIC CLOVE, MINCED

3½ POUNDS FRESH SPINACH (OR 1 POUND FROZEN, THAWED)

1 TEASPOON SEA SALT

½ TEASPOON BLACK PEPPER

¼ TEASPOON GROUND NUTMEG

1 CUP CRUMBLED FETA CHEESE

6 BONELESS, SKINLESS CHICKEN BREAST HALVES

½ CUP DRY WHITE WINE

2 CUPS CHICKEN STOCK

continued ▶

Spinach and Feta–Stuffed Chicken Breasts with Lemon-Dill Sauce *continued* ▶

LEMON-DILL SAUCE
2 TABLESPOONS UNSALTED BUTTER
2 TABLESPOONS ALL-PURPOSE FLOUR
1½ CUPS CHICKEN STOCK
1 CUP HEAVY CREAM
ZEST OF 1 LEMON
2 TABLESPOONS FRESH LEMON JUICE
¼ CUP CHOPPED FRESH DILL
SEA SALT
BLACK PEPPER

To make the stuffed chicken:

1. In a large skillet, heat the olive oil over medium-high heat. Add the shallot and garlic and sauté for 2 minutes, or until the shallot is slightly softened.

2. Add the spinach, 1 teaspoon salt, ½ teaspoon black pepper, and the nutmeg to the skillet. Sauté the spinach until the liquid in the pan has evaporated and the spinach is dry. Remove to a medium bowl, cool the mixture slightly, and stir in the feta cheese. Set aside.

3. On a cutting board, spread out a piece of parchment paper as large as the board. Trim the chicken breasts of any excess fat, and lay one breast shiny-side (skin-side) down on the parchment paper. Place another piece of parchment paper over the chicken, and pound with a meat pounder, flat-bottom bottle, or rolling pin to an even thickness, about ½ inch. Repeat with the 5 remaining chicken breast halves.

4. Lay a chicken breast half on the work surface and season with salt and pepper. Place about 2 tablespoons of the spinach-feta filling in the center of the breast. Roll up the breast, beginning at the widest end and tucking in the sides, and secure with a toothpick. Repeat with the remaining chicken breasts and filling.

5. In the skillet over medium-high heat, brown the stuffed chicken breasts in the remaining olive oil in batches, transferring them to the slow cooker when they are browned around all sides.

6. Add the wine to the skillet, scraping up the flavorful browned bits from the bottom of the pan. Pour the wine and the chicken stock into the slow cooker.

7. Cover and cook on high for 2½ hours or on low for 4 to 5 hours, until the chicken is cooked through and registers 160°F on a meat thermometer.

8. Using tongs, remove the chicken from the slow cooker, arrange on a cutting board, and cover with parchment paper. Allow the chicken to rest for 5 minutes. Cut each chicken breast half on the bias into three pieces, and serve in a pool of the lemon-dill sauce.

To make the lemon-dill sauce:

1. In a medium skillet, melt the butter over medium heat. Whisk in the flour. Cook, whisking constantly. When white bubbles form, cook for another 2 to 3 minutes, still whisking.

2. Gradually add the broth, whisking until it comes to a boil and the mixture is smooth and thickened.

3. Stir in the cream, lemon zest, lemon juice, and dill. Season with salt and pepper.

4. Serve hot, or cool to room temperature and refrigerate for up to 4 days. Gently reheat over low heat before serving.

Bell Pepper and Tomato Chicken

SERVES 6 TO 8

This simple recipe is wonderful over pasta, or if you want a lighter meal, over spaghetti squash. This kind of dish is a tastier and much healthier alternative to jarred pasta sauces.

1 MEDIUM YELLOW ONION, SLICED THICKLY

1 BELL PEPPER, ANY COLOR, CORED, SEEDED, AND SLICED THICKLY

4 CLOVES GARLIC, MINCED

6 OUNCES PITTED BLACK OLIVES, DRAINED

ONE 28-OUNCE CAN STEWED TOMATOES

ONE 15-OUNCE CAN STEWED TOMATOES

ONE 6-OUNCE CAN TOMATO PASTE

1 CUP RED OR WHITE WINE

2 TABLESPOONS LEMON JUICE

4 TO 6 BONELESS, SKINLESS CHICKEN BREASTS, CUT IN HALF

¼ CUP CHOPPED FRESH PARSLEY, OR 2 TABLESPOONS DRIED PARSLEY

1 TABLESPOON DRIED BASIL

½ TEASPOON GROUND NUTMEG

SEA SALT

BLACK PEPPER

1 TABLESPOON RED PEPPER FLAKES (OPTIONAL)

1. Place the onion, bell pepper, garlic, and olives in slow cooker.

2. Add the stewed tomatoes, tomato paste, wine, and lemon juice. Stir to combine.

3. Place the chicken pieces in the slow cooker. Make sure all the pieces are covered with the liquid.

4. Sprinkle with the parsley, basil, and nutmeg. Season with salt and black pepper, and add the red pepper flakes, if using. Cover and cook on high for 5 hours or on low for 8 hours. Make sure the chicken is cooked thoroughly.

5. Serve hot over cooked pasta of your choice or cooked spaghetti squash.

Provençal Chicken Supper

SERVES 4

This dish from the French countryside comes together in minutes. Add some vegetables or a salad on the side as well as some crusty bread for an authentic, delicious, simple meal.

FOUR 6-OUNCE BONELESS, SKINLESS CHICKEN BREAST HALVES

2 TEASPOONS DRIED BASIL

1 TEASPOON DRIED OREGANO

½ TEASPOON SEA SALT

¼ TEASPOON BLACK PEPPER

1 YELLOW BELL PEPPER, DICED

2 CLOVES GARLIC, MINCED

ONE 15-OUNCE CAN CANNELLINI BEANS, RINSED AND DRAINED

ONE 15-OUNCE CAN DICED TOMATOES, WITH THE JUICE

4 BASIL SPRIGS, FOR GARNISH

1. Place the chicken in the slow cooker. Sprinkle with the basil, oregano, salt, and black pepper. Add the bell pepper, garlic, cannellini beans, and tomatoes.

2. Cover and cook on low for 8 hours until the chicken is cooked thoroughly.

3. Serve hot, garnished with a basil sprig.

Sweet Glazed Chicken Thighs

SERVES 6

This very easy chicken dish becomes even tastier when prepared in a slow cooker. The sweetness of the pineapple juice and the subtle tanginess of the vinegar are a fantastic combination. Serve with hot quinoa or rice.

NONSTICK COOKING OIL SPRAY

2 POUNDS SKINLESS, BONELESS CHICKEN THIGHS

½ TEASPOON BLACK PEPPER

¼ TEASPOON DRIED SALT

1 TEASPOON OLIVE OIL

1 CUP PINEAPPLE JUICE

2 TABLESPOONS LIGHT BROWN SUGAR

1½ TABLESPOONS WORCESTERSHIRE SAUCE

1 TABLESPOON WHITE WINE

1 TABLESPOON BALSAMIC VINEGAR

3 TABLESPOONS WATER

2 TABLESPOONS CORNSTARCH

3 CUPS HOT COOKED QUINOA OR RICE, FOR SERVING

3 TABLESPOONS SLICED GREEN ONIONS, FOR SERVING

1. Coat the interior of the slow cooker crock with cooking oil spray.

2. Sprinkle the chicken with pepper and salt.

3. Heat a large nonstick skillet over medium-high heat. Add the oil and swirl to coat.

4. Add the chicken to pan. Cook 2 to 3 minutes on each side or until browned. Transfer the chicken to the slow cooker.

5. Stir the pineapple juice and vinegar into the drippings in the skillet, scraping the pan with a wooden spoon to loosen the flavorful browned bits. Remove from the heat.

6. Stir in the brown sugar, Worcestershire sauce, and white wine. Pour the juice mixture over the chicken in the slow cooker.

7. Cover the slow cooker and cook on low for 2½ hours.

8. Transfer the chicken to a serving platter with a slotted spoon. Increase the slow cooker heat to high.

9. Combine the 3 tablespoons water and the cornstarch in a small bowl. Add to the sauce in the slow cooker, stirring with a whisk. Cook 2 minutes or until sauce thickens, stirring constantly with a whisk.

10. Place rice on each of six plates. Top with the chicken thighs and the sauce. Sprinkle each serving with the green onions.

Chicken Jambalaya

SERVES 8

Originating in the Caribbean, where the Spanish and islander cultures mixed, jambalaya is traditionally made in three parts. First, meat and vegetables are added together and cooked, blending their flavors, and then the dish is finished once stock and rice are added. Jambalaya is very similar to its Mediterranean relative, the paella eaten in Spain.

1 TABLESPOON OLIVE OIL

1 POUND SKINLESS, BONELESS CHICKEN BREASTS, CUT INTO 1-INCH PIECES

¾ POUND SKINLESS, BONELESS CHICKEN THIGHS, CUT INTO 1-INCH PIECES

2 LARGE YELLOW ONIONS, CHOPPED

1 LARGE GREEN BELL PEPPER, CHOPPED

1 LARGE STALK CELERY, CHOPPED

2 GARLIC CLOVES, MINCED

4 OUNCES TURKEY KIELBASA, HALVED AND CUT INTO ¼-INCH SLICES

ONE 28-OUNCE CAN DICED TOMATOES, WITH THE JUICE

2 CUPS CHICKEN STOCK

1 TEASPOON GARLIC POWDER

1 TEASPOON PAPRIKA

½ TEASPOON ONION POWDER

½ TEASPOON CAYENNE PEPPER

½ TEASPOON DRIED OREGANO

½ TEASPOON DRIED THYME

½ TEASPOON BLACK PEPPER

¼ TEASPOON SPANISH SMOKED PAPRIKA

1 CUP UNCOOKED LONG-GRAIN RICE

2 TABLESPOONS CHOPPED FRESH FLAT-LEAF PARSLEY

1 TABLESPOON HOT PEPPER SAUCE (LIKE TABASCO)

1. Heat a large skillet over medium-high heat. Add the olive oil and swirl to coat. Add the chicken and cook 4 minutes, stirring occasionally. Place the chicken in slow cooker.

2. In the large skillet, add the onions, bell pepper, celery, and garlic. Sauté 4 minutes or until the vegetables are tender.

3. Add the onion mixture, turkey kielbasa, tomatoes, and chicken stock to the slow cooker. Sprinkle with the garlic powder, paprika, onion powder, cayenne pepper, oregano, thyme, black pepper, and Spanish smoked paprika. Cover and cook on low for 5 hours.

4. Cook the rice according to the package directions. Add the cooked rice, parsley, and hot pepper sauce to the slow cooker. Cover and cook on high 15 minutes. Serve hot.

Chicken-Green Olive Stew

SERVES 4

The olives and almonds make this dish, so don't leave them out. This stew goes perfectly over couscous, but feel free to serve it over the starch of your choice. Rice, farro, and quinoa are also good options.

ONE 28-OUNCE CAN DICED TOMATOES, DRAINED
1 CUP CHICKEN STOCK
1 LARGE YELLOW ONION, SLICED
1 GARLIC CLOVE, MINCED
1 TEASPOON GROUND CUMIN
1 TEASPOON PAPRIKA
½ TEASPOON GROUND TURMERIC
1 TABLESPOON OLIVE OIL
ONE 3-POUND SKINLESS QUARTERED CHICKEN
½ TEASPOON BLACK PEPPER
¼ TEASPOON SEA SALT
½ CUP RED WINE
½ CUP PITTED GREEN OLIVES
ZEST OF 1 LEMON
2 CUPS HOT COOKED COUSCOUS
¼ CUP SLICED ALMONDS, TOASTED

1. Place the tomatoes, stock, onion, and garlic into the slow cooker. Sprinkle in the cumin, paprika, and turmeric.

2. Heat a large skillet over medium-high heat. Add the olive oil and swirl to coat the pan.

3. Sprinkle the chicken with the pepper and salt. Add the chicken to pan. Cook the chicken about 8 minutes, browning on all sides. Place in the slow cooker.

4. Pour the wine into the skillet, scraping the pan with a wooden spoon to loosen the flavorful browned bits on the bottom. Pour the liquid into the slow cooker.

5. Cover and cook on high for 4 hours. At 30 minutes before the end of the cooking time, stir in the olives and lemon zest.

6. Remove the chicken from the slow cooker, place on a plate, and cool. Remove the meat from the bones and return it to the slow cooker. Discard bones.

7. Serve the chicken stew hot over the couscous, and sprinkle with the toasted almonds.

Chicken Cacciatore

SERVES 8

Cacciatore is the Italian word for "hunter," and this dish made with tomatoes, mushrooms, onions, and red wine was traditionally a rustic vehicle for game. Today it remains a simple and delicious way to eat whatever meat you have, but poultry is especially well-suited for this dish.

8 BONE-IN SKINLESS CHICKEN THIGHS

8 BONE-IN SKINLESS CHICKEN DRUMSTICKS

1 TEASPOON SEA SALT

½ TEASPOON BLACK PEPPER

1 TABLESPOON OLIVE OIL

NONSTICK COOKING OIL SPRAY

8 OUNCES CREMINI MUSHROOMS, QUARTERED

2 TABLESPOONS GARLIC, MINCED

1 LARGE YELLOW ONION, SLICED

1 GREEN BELL PEPPER, CUT INTO STRIPS

1 RED BELL PEPPER, CUT INTO STRIPS

½ CUP DRY WHITE WINE

⅓ CUP ALL-PURPOSE FLOUR

2 TABLESPOONS CHOPPED FRESH OREGANO

2 TABLESPOONS CHOPPED FRESH THYME, PLUS MORE FOR GARNISH

ONE 28-OUNCE CAN WHOLE PLUM TOMATOES, CHOPPED AND WITH THE JUICE

4 CUPS HOT COOKED FETTUCCINE

1. Sprinkle the chicken with ½ teaspoon salt and the black pepper.

2. Heat a large nonstick skillet over medium-high heat. Add the oil to the pan and swirl to coat.

3. Add half of the chicken to the pan. Cook 5 minutes on each side or until lightly browned. Coat the slow cooker with cooking oil spray. Place the chicken in the slow cooker. Repeat with remaining chicken.

4. Place the mushrooms on top of the chicken.

5. Return the skillet to the heat. Add the garlic, onion, and yellow, green, and red bell peppers. Sprinkle with the remaining ½ teaspoon salt. Reduce the heat to medium, and cook, stirring often, for 5 minutes or until the vegetables are crisp-tender.

6. Add the wine, and with a wooden spoon stir to loosen the flavorful browned bits from the bottom of the pan. Cook 1 minute.

7. Stir in the flour. Stir in the oregano, thyme, and tomatoes. Cook for 1 minute, stirring frequently.

8. Pour the tomato mixture over the mushrooms in the slow cooker.

9. Cover and cook on low for 3 hours or until the chicken is very tender.

10. Serve hot over fettuccine. Sprinkle with additional thyme, if desired.

Sweet and Spicy Chicken

SERVES 6

This tasty dish is simple to prepare, but the flavors are complex. Even if a touch of sweetness in a meat dish is unfamiliar to you, give this recipe a try, as it may well win you over. Serve over rice, pasta, or even on bread.

2 TEASPOONS GROUND CUMIN

½ TEASPOON GROUND CINNAMON

¾ TEASPOON COARSE SEA SALT

½ TEASPOON BLACK PEPPER

4 CHICKEN LEG QUARTERS

1 TABLESPOON EXTRA-VIRGIN OLIVE OIL

1 MEDIUM YELLOW ONION, CUT INTO ½-INCH WEDGES (ROOT END LEFT INTACT)

3 GARLIC CLOVES, MINCED

3-INCH PIECE FRESH PEELED GINGER, SLICED INTO ROUNDS

ONE 28-OUNCE CAN DICED TOMATOES, WITH THE JUICE

½ CUP RAISINS

1. In a large resealable plastic bag, combine the cumin, cinnamon, salt, and black pepper. Add the chicken to the bag, reseal, and toss to coat.

2. In a large skillet over medium-high heat, heat the olive oil. Add the chicken, skin-side down, and cook until golden, about 4 minutes. Turn and cook 2 additional minutes.

3. Place the onion, garlic, and ginger in the slow cooker.

4. Add the chicken, skin-side up, to slow cooker. Top the chicken with the tomatoes and raisins.

5. Cover and cook until chicken is tender, 3½ hours on high or 6 hours on low. Serve hot.

Garlic Chicken with Couscous

SERVES 4

Don't be intimidated by cooking with a whole chicken. There are many step-by-step guides that can help you cut them, and you can save lots of money by buying this way, especially when your recipe calls for the various pieces as this one does. You'll likely get the knack of it pretty quickly, or you can ask the butcher to cut up a chicken for you.

1 WHOLE CHICKEN, 3½ TO 4 POUNDS, CUT INTO 6 TO 8 PIECES AND PATTED DRY
COARSE SEA SALT
BLACK PEPPER
1 TABLESPOON EXTRA-VIRGIN OLIVE OIL
1 MEDIUM YELLOW ONION, HALVED AND THINLY SLICED
6 CLOVES GARLIC, HALVED
2 TEASPOONS DRIED THYME
1 CUP DRY WHITE WINE
⅓ CUP ALL-PURPOSE FLOUR
1 CUP UNCOOKED COUSCOUS
¼ CHOPPED FRESH PARSLEY

1. Season the chicken with salt and pepper.

2. In a large skillet, heat the oil over medium-high heat. Add the chicken skin-side down and cook in batches until the skin is golden brown, about 4 minutes. Turn and cook an additional 2 minutes.

3. Add the onion, garlic, and thyme to the slow cooker.

4. Top the contents of slow cooker with chicken, skin-side up, in a tight layer.

5. In a small bowl, whisk together the wine and the flour until smooth, and add to the slow cooker.

6. Cover and cook until the chicken is tender, about 3½ hours on high or 7 hours on low.

7. Cook the couscous according to package instructions.

8. Serve the chicken and sauce hot over the couscous, sprinkled with parsley.

Whole Roast Chicken with Potatoes

SERVES 4

Even if you've never roasted a whole chicken, take heart! The slow cooker is actually the break you've been waiting for. This is easy as can be, and the chicken will stay moist—in fact, the meat will be fall-off-the-bone tender. Just check that your slow cooker can accommodate both a whole chicken and potatoes before you attempt to cook them all at once.

4 TO 6 YUKON GOLD POTATOES, QUARTERED

1 WHOLE SKINLESS CHICKEN, 4 TO 5 POUNDS

1 LARGE YELLOW ONION, QUARTERED

4 OR 5 CLOVES GARLIC, WHOLE

2 TEASPOONS SEA SALT

1 TEASPOON PAPRIKA

1 TEASPOON ONION POWDER

½ TEASPOON DRIED THYME

1 TEASPOON DRIED OREGANO

1 TEASPOON DRIED ROSEMARY

½ TEASPOON DRIED PARSLEY

½ TEASPOON CAYENNE PEPPER

½ TEASPOON BLACK PEPPER

1. Place the potatoes in the slow cooker.

2. Clean out the chicken cavity. Rinse the chicken, inside and out. Pat dry.

3. Stuff the cavity with the onion and garlic.

4. In a small bowl, combine the salt, paprika, onion powder, thyme, oregano, rosemary, parsley, cayenne pepper, and black pepper. Rub the mixture all over the chicken.

5. Place the chicken over the potatoes in the slow cooker, breast-side down.

6. Cook on high for 4 to 5 hours, or on low for 8 hours.

7. When serving, spoon up some of the juice on the bottom of the slow cooker and ladle over the chicken.

Moroccan Chicken with Apricots, Almonds, and Olives

SERVES 4

The coriander and cumin, in particular, among the spices in this dish, lend it aroma and flavor that are unique to Moroccan cuisine. Accompanied by dried apricots, chickpeas, and toasted almonds, this dish provides all of the typical flavors of this Mediterranean region.

3 POUNDS SKINLESS CHICKEN THIGHS

1 YELLOW ONION, CUT INTO ½-INCH WEDGES

1 TEASPOON GROUND CUMIN

½ TEASPOON GROUND GINGER

½ TEASPOON GROUND CORIANDER

¼ TEASPOON GROUND CINNAMON

¼ TEASPOON CAYENNE PEPPER

SEA SALT

BLACK PEPPER

1 BAY LEAF

⅓ CUP CHICKEN STOCK

ONE 15-OUNCE CAN CHICKPEAS, DRAINED AND RINSED

½ CUP GREEN OLIVES

½ CUP DRIED TURKISH APRICOTS

⅓ CUP SLICED ALMONDS, TOASTED

1. In a large bowl, mix the chicken thighs and the onion. Add the cumin, coriander, ginger, cinnamon, and cayenne and toss to coat. Season the spiced chicken and onion with salt and pepper.

2. Transfer the chicken and onion to the slow cooker. Add the bay leaf and chicken stock to the slow cooker.

3. Cover and cook on high for 2 hours.

continued ▶

Moroccan Chicken with Apricots, Almonds, and Olives *continued* ▶

4. Stir in the chickpeas, olives, and apricots. Cover and cook until the chicken is tender and cooked through and the apricots are plump, about 1 hour more.

5. Remove the bay leaf and season the juices with salt and pepper.

6. Meanwhile, preheat the oven to 350°F. Spread the almonds in a pie plate and toast for about 7 minutes, until fragrant and lightly golden. Watch them so they don't burn.

7. Spoon the hot chicken, vegetables, and juices into shallow bowls, sprinkle with the toasted almonds, and serve.

Catalonian Chicken with Spiced Lemon Rice

SERVES 4

You may have a tough time deciding what you like better about this dish: the savory chicken or the slightly spicy rice. Don't worry, you can keep trying it and decide later!

3 TABLESPOONS ALL-PURPOSE FLOUR

2 TABLESPOONS PAPRIKA

1 TABLESPOON GARLIC POWDER

SEA SALT

BLACK PEPPER

6 CHICKEN THIGHS

¼ CUP OLIVE OIL

ONE 15-OUNCE CAN DICED TOMATOES, WITH THE JUICE

2 GREEN BELL PEPPERS, DICED INTO 2-INCH PIECES

1 LARGE YELLOW ONION, SLICED INTO THICK PIECES

2 TABLESPOONS TOMATO PASTE

4 CUPS CHICKEN STOCK

1 CUP UNCOOKED RICE (BROWN OR WHITE)

½ TEASPOON RED PEPPER FLAKES

ZEST AND JUICE FROM 1 LEMON

½ CUP PITTED GREEN OLIVES

1. In a large resealable bag, mix together the flour, paprika, and garlic powder and season with salt and pepper. Add the chicken, reseal the bag, and toss to coat.

2. In a large skillet over medium heat, heat the olive oil. Add the chicken and brown on both sides, 3 to 4 minutes per side.

3. While the chicken is cooking, add the tomatoes, bell peppers, and onion to the slow cooker.

4. Place the browned chicken thighs in the slow cooker.

continued ▶

Catalonian Chicken with Spiced Lemon Rice *continued* ▶

5. In same skillet used to brown the chicken, add the tomato paste and cook for 1 minute, stirring constantly.

6. Add 2 cups of the chicken stock to the skillet and bring to a simmer, stirring with a wooden spoon to scrape up the flavorful browned bits off the bottom of the pan. Pour over the top of the chicken in the slow cooker.

7. Cook on low for 4 hours, or until the chicken is extremely tender.

8. In a heavy medium saucepan over medium-high heat, combine the remaining 2 cups stock, the rice, red pepper flakes, lemon zest, and juice of one-half of the lemon, and season with salt. Bring to a boil, reduce the heat to low, and simmer, covered, until the rice is tender and has absorbed all the liquid, about 25 minutes.

9. To serve, spoon the rice onto plates and ladle the Catalonian chicken and vegetables over the top. Garnish with the olives and squeeze the juice from the remaining one-half lemon over the dish.

Greek-Style Roast Turkey Breast

SERVES 8

If you shop for Greek seasoning blends and check their ingredients, you'll notice that no two brands have the same blend of spices in them. Greek cuisine is heavy on spice use, and this dish makes use of several spices that you may find unusual—until you taste them in action!

ONE 4-POUND TURKEY BREAST, TRIMMED OF FAT
½ CUP CHICKEN STOCK
2 TABLESPOONS FRESH LEMON JUICE
2 CUPS CHOPPED ONIONS
½ CUP PITTED KALAMATA OLIVES
½ CUP OIL-PACKED SUN-DRIED TOMATOES, DRAINED AND THINLY SLICED
1 CLOVE GARLIC, MINCED
1 TEASPOON DRIED OREGANO
½ TEASPOON GROUND CINNAMON
½ TEASPOON GROUND DILL
¼ TEASPOON GROUND NUTMEG
¼ TEASPOON CAYENNE PEPPER
1 TEASPOON SEA SALT
¼ TEASPOON BLACK PEPPER
3 TABLESPOONS ALL-PURPOSE FLOUR

1. Place the turkey breast, ¼ cup of the chicken stock, lemon juice, onions, Kalamata olives, garlic, and sun-dried tomatoes into the slow cooker. Sprinkle with the oregano, cinnamon, dill, nutmeg, cayenne pepper, salt, and black pepper. Cover and cook on low for 7 hours.

2. Combine the remaining ¼ cup chicken stock and the flour in a small bowl. Whisk until smooth. Stir into the slow cooker. Cover and cook on low for an additional 30 minutes.

3. Serve hot over rice, pasta, potatoes, or another starch of your choice.

Pheasant with Mushrooms and Olives

SERVES 6

Pheasant is a traditional Italian food, and this kind of game bird can be found in Italian markets, ready for cooking. This recipe can be adapted for use with other game birds, or even for chicken.

2 TABLESPOONS OLIVE OIL
¾ CUP ALL-PURPOSE FLOUR
1 TEASPOON SEA SALT
¼ TEASPOON BLACK PEPPER
2 PHEASANTS, RINSED, PATTED DRY, AND CUT INTO BITE-SIZE PIECES
1 YELLOW ONION, SLICED AND SEPARATED INTO RINGS
1 CUP CREMINI MUSHROOMS, SLICED
3 CLOVES GARLIC, MINCED
1 CUP DRY WHITE WINE
1 CUP CHICKEN STOCK
½ CUP SLICED BLACK OLIVES

1. Place the flour, salt, and pepper into a resealable plastic bag, and shake to combine.

2. Place the pheasant pieces into the bag with the flour mixture, and shake until evenly coated.

3. Heat the olive oil in a large skillet over medium-high heat.

4. Shake any excess flour off of the pheasant pieces, and place them in the hot oil. Cook until the pheasant is brown on both sides, about 6 minutes.

5. Place the pheasant into the slow cooker, reserving the oil in the skillet.

6. Add the onion and cook in the remaining oil in the skillet until it softens, about 3 minutes.

7. Stir the mushrooms and garlic into the oil and onion, and continue cooking and stirring until the mushrooms have softened and the garlic has mellowed, about 5 minutes more.

8. Pour the wine into the skillet and bring to a boil. Boil for 5 minutes; then pour in the chicken stock and return to a boil.

9. Pour the mushroom mixture into the slow cooker, and sprinkle with the sliced black olives.

10. Cover and cook on high for 4 hours or on low for 7 hours. Serve hot.

CHAPTER EIGHT

Meat

There's no substitute for the heartiest of meat dishes, and the slow cooker is the perfect place for them. Even the toughest of cuts are transformed into tender, succulent masterpieces when prepared in a slow cooker. Here's your chance to tackle dishes you've never tried before, like pork loin, lamb shanks, or osso buco—this chapter will show you how.

Lamb Tagine

SERVES 6

A tagine, named for the kind of vessel it is cooked in, is a type of slow-cooked Moroccan stew. Lamb is the most common kind of meat used in tagines, and typically cheaper cuts such as the shoulder or shank are used since the slow cooking process tenderizes even the most stubborn cuts. Here, dates and saffron lend the dish color and flavor as well as enough flair for a formal dinner.

1 NAVEL ORANGE

2 TABLESPOONS ALL-PURPOSE FLOUR

2 POUNDS BONELESS LEG OF LAMB, TRIMMED AND CUT INTO 1½-INCH CUBES

½ CUP CHICKEN STOCK

2 LARGE WHITE ONIONS, CHOPPED

1 TEASPOON PUMPKIN PIE SPICE

1 TEASPOON GROUND CUMIN

½ TEASPOON SEA SALT

¼ TEASPOON SAFFRON THREADS, CRUSHED IN YOUR PALM

¼ TEASPOON GROUND RED PEPPER

1 CUP PITTED DATES

2 TABLESPOONS HONEY

3 CUPS HOT COOKED COUSCOUS, FOR SERVING

2 TABLESPOONS TOASTED SLIVERED ALMONDS, FOR SERVING

1. Grate 2 teaspoons of zest from the orange into a small bowl. Squeeze ¼ cup juice from the orange into another small bowl.

2. Add the flour to the orange juice, stirring with a whisk until smooth. Stir in the orange zest.

3. Heat a large nonstick skillet over medium-high heat. Add the lamb and sauté 7 minutes or until browned. Stir in the stock, scraping the bottom of the pan with a wooden spoon to loosen the flavorful brown bits. Stir in the orange juice mixture.

4. Stir the onions into the lamb mixture. Add the pumpkin pie spice, cumin, salt, saffron, and ground red pepper.

5. Pour the lamb mixture into the slow cooker. Cover and cook on low for 6 hours or until the lamb is tender.

6. Stir the dates and honey into the lamb mixture. Cover and cook on low for 1 hour or until thoroughly heated.

7. Serve the lamb tagine over the couscous and sprinkle with the almonds.

Tarragon Lamb Shanks with Cannellini Beans

SERVES 12

The shank on lamb is one of the toughest cuts, so it is perfect for slow cooking, with beans, root vegetables, and stronger herbs like tarragon. Don't forget to rinse the canned beans to reduce their sodium content.

FOUR 1½-POUND LAMB SHANKS

ONE 19-OUNCE CAN CANNELLINI OR OTHER WHITE BEANS, RINSED AND DRAINED

2 MEDIUM-SIZED CARROTS, DICED

1 LARGE YELLOW ONION, CHOPPED

1 LARGE STALK CELERY, CHOPPED

2 CLOVES GARLIC, THINLY SLICED

2 TEASPOONS TARRAGON

½ TEASPOON SEA SALT

¼ TEASPOON BLACK PEPPER

ONE 28-OUNCE CAN DICED TOMATOES, WITH THE JUICE

1. Trim the fat from the lamb shanks.

2. Put the beans, carrots, onion, celery, and garlic in the slow cooker and stir to combine.

3. Place lamb shanks on the bean mixture, and sprinkle with the tarragon, salt, and pepper.

4. Pour the tomatoes over the lamb. Cover and cook on high for 1 hour.

5. Reduce heat to low, and cook 9 hours or until the lamb is very tender. Remove the lamb shanks from slow cooker and place on a plate.

6. Pour the bean mixture through a colander or sieve over a bowl, reserving the liquid. Let the liquid stand for 5 minutes. Skim the fat from the surface of the liquid. Return the bean mixture to the liquid. Return to the slow cooker.

7. Remove the lamb from the bones. Discard the bones. Return the lamb to the slow cooker. Cover and cook to reheat, about 15 minutes.

8. Serve the lamb hot with the bean mixture.

Lamb with Olives and Potatoes

SERVES 4

Lamb shanks are perfect for gentle, slow cooking. To ensure that the lamb shanks fit into your slow cooker, you can always ask the butcher to slice them. The simple, rustic flavors of this dish—olives, potatoes, rosemary, white wine—are the ideal combination to make the most of this cut of lamb and the cooking process.

1¼ POUNDS SMALL POTATOES, HALVED

4 LARGE SHALLOTS, CUT INTO ½-INCH WEDGES

3 CLOVES GARLIC, MINCED

1 TABLESPOON LEMON ZEST

3 SPRIGS FRESH ROSEMARY

COARSE SEA SALT

BLACK PEPPER

4 TABLESPOONS ALL-PURPOSE FLOUR

¾ CUP CHICKEN STOCK

3½ POUNDS LAMB SHANKS, CUT CROSSWISE INTO 1½-INCH PIECES AND FAT TRIMMED

2 TABLESPOONS EXTRA-VIRGIN OLIVE OIL

½ CUP DRY WHITE WINE

1 CUP PITTED GREEN OLIVES, HALVED

2 TABLESPOONS LEMON JUICE

1. Combine the potatoes, shallots, garlic, lemon zest, and rosemary sprigs in the slow cooker. Season with salt and pepper.

2. In a small bowl, whisk together 1 tablespoon of the flour and the stock. Add to the slow cooker.

3. Place the remaining 3 tablespoons flour on a plate. Season the lamb with salt and pepper; then coat in the flour, shaking off any excess.

4. In a large skillet over medium-high, heat the olive oil. In batches, cook the lamb until browned on all sides, about 10 minutes. Transfer to the slow cooker.

continued ▶

Lamb with Olives and Potatoes *continued* ▶

5. Add the wine to the skillet and cook, stiring with a wooden spoon and scraping up the flavorful browned bits from the bottom of the pan, until reduced by half, about 2 minutes. Then add to the slow cooker.

6. Cover and cook until the lamb is tender, on high for about 3½ hours, or on low for 7 hours.

7. Stir in olive halves, then cover, and cook 20 additional minutes.

8. To serve, transfer the lamb and vegetables to warm plates.

9. Skim the fat from the cooking liquid, then stir in the lemon juice, and season the sauce with salt and pepper.

10. Serve the sauce with the lamb and vegetables.

Lamb Shanks and Potatoes

SERVES 6

This dish comes together in minutes, and then fills your house with a delicious aroma for hours. The apricot jam lends a bright Mediterranean note that goes perfectly with lamb and rosemary.

ONE 15-OUNCE CAN CRUSHED TOMATOES IN PURÉE

3 TABLESPOONS TOMATO PASTE

2 TABLESPOONS APRICOT JAM

6 CLOVES GARLIC, THINLY SLICED

3 STRIPS ORANGE ZEST

¾ TEASPOON CRUSHED DRIED ROSEMARY

½ TEASPOON GROUND GINGER

½ TEASPOON GROUND CINNAMON

COARSE SEA SALT

BLACK PEPPER

3½ POUNDS LAMB SHANKS, TRIMMED OF EXCESS FAT AND CUT INTO 1½-INCH SLICES

1¼ POUNDS SMALL NEW POTATOES, HALVED (OR QUARTERED, IF LARGE)

1. Stir together the tomatoes and purée, tomato paste, jam, garlic, orange zest, rosemary, ginger, and cinnamon in the slow cooker. Season with salt and pepper.

2. Add the lamb and potatoes, and spoon the tomato mixture over the lamb to coat.

3. Cover and cook until the lamb and potatoes are tender, on low for 8 hours or on high for 5 hours. Season again with salt and pepper, if desired.

4. Serve hot.

Braised Pork Loin with Port and Dried Plums

SERVES 10

Pork tenderloin is among the leanest cuts of meats available. That's where your slow cooker comes in, and with this recipe, it's never been easier to cook pork loin roast to tasty perfection.

ONE 3¼-POUND BONELESS PORK LOIN ROAST, TRIMMED

1½ TEASPOONS BLACK PEPPER

1 TEASPOON SEA SALT

1 TEASPOON DRY MUSTARD

1 TEASPOON DRIED SAGE

½ TEASPOON DRIED THYME

1 TABLESPOON OLIVE OIL

2 LARGE YELLOW ONIONS, SLICED

1 CUP FINELY CHOPPED LEEK, WHITE AND LIGHT GREEN PARTS, RINSED

1 LARGE CARROT, FINELY CHOPPED

½ CUP PORT OR OTHER SWEET RED WINE

⅔ CUP CHICKEN STOCK

1 CUP PITTED DRIED PLUMS (ABOUT 20)

2 BAY LEAVES

2 TABLESPOONS CORNSTARCH

2 TABLESPOONS WATER

1. Cut the pork roast in half crosswise.

2. Combine the pepper, salt, dry mustard, sage, and thyme in a small bowl. Rub the seasoning mixture over the surface of the roast halves.

3. Heat a Dutch oven over medium-high heat. Add the olive oil to pan and swirl to coat. Add the pork and brown on all sides, about 4 minutes. Place the pork in the slow cooker.

4. Add the onions, leek, and carrot to the Dutch oven, and sauté for 5 minutes or until vegetables are golden.

5. Stir in the wine and stock, and cook for about 1 minute, scraping the bottom of the pan with a wooden spoon to loosen up the flavorful browned bits.

6. Pour the wine-vegetable mixture over the pork in slow cooker. Add the plums and bay leaves.

7. Cover and cook on high for 1 hour. Reduce the heat to low, and cook for 5 to 6 hours, or until the pork is tender.

8. Remove the pork from the slow cooker, set aside on a platter, and keep warm. Increase the heat to high.

9. Combine the cornstarch and 2 tablespoons water in a small bowl. Whisk to combine, and then whisk into the cooking liquid in the slow cooker.

10. Cook, uncovered, for 15 minutes or until the sauce is thick, stirring frequently.

11. Discard the bay leaves. Slice the pork, and serve hot with the sauce.

Italian Braised Pork

SERVES 4

This dish makes use of pork shoulder, the standard cut for tender, shredded pork dishes such as pulled pork. Here, the pork is served over couscous, but it is just as tasty with pasta or rice— or even left over in a sandwich.

2½ POUNDS BONELESS PORK SHOULDER

COARSE SEA SALT

BLACK PEPPER

2 TABLESPOONS OLIVE OIL

1 LARGE YELLOW ONION, FINELY DICED

3 CLOVES GARLIC, MINCED

1 STALK CELERY, FINELY DICED

¾ TEASPOON FENNEL SEEDS

½ CUP DRY RED WINE

ONE 28-OUNCE CAN CRUSHED TOMATOES

4 CUPS PREPARED HOT COUSCOUS, FOR SERVING

1. Season the pork with salt and pepper.

2. In a large skillet, heat the olive oil over medium-high heat. Cook the pork, turning occasionally, until browned on all sides, about 8 minutes. Transfer the pork to the slow cooker.

3. Reduce the heat under the skillet to medium, and add the onion, garlic, celery, and fennel seeds. Cook, stirring often, until the onion is softened, about 4 minutes.

4. Add the wine and cook, stirring with a wooden spoon and scraping up the flavorful browned bits from the bottom of the pan, until the liquid is reduced by half, about 2 minutes. Add the wine mixture to the slow cooker, and stir in the tomatoes.

5. Cover and cook on high for 4 hours, or until the pork is very tender, or on low for 8 hours.

6. Transfer the pork to a cutting board. Shred the meat into bite-size pieces. Discard any pieces of fat.

7. Skim the fat off the sauce in the slow cooker and discard. Return the shredded pork to the slow cooker and stir to combine. Cook the pork and sauce for 5 minutes to reheat.

8. Serve hot over the couscous.

Sausage Lasagna

SERVES 8

To fit lasagna noodles into a round slow cooker, just break them up. There's no need to precook the noodles: When the rest of the lasagna is done, the noodles will also be ready.

1 POUND ITALIAN PORK SAUSAGE, CASINGS REMOVED

1 POUND GROUND BEEF SIRLOIN

1 MEDIUM YELLOW ONION, FINELY CHOPPED

2 MEDIUM CARROTS, FINELY CHOPPED

2 CLOVES GARLIC, MINCED

COARSE SEA SALT

BLACK PEPPER

ONE 6-OUNCE CAN TOMATO PASTE

ONE 28-OUNCE CAN CRUSHED TOMATOES IN PURÉE

9 LASAGNA NOODLES

2 CUPS SHREDDED PART-SKIM MOZZARELLA CHEESE (ABOUT 8 OUNCES)

1. In a 5-quart Dutch oven or large heavy pot, cook the sausage and beef over medium-high, breaking up the meat with a wooden spoon. Cook, stirring often, until no longer pink, 4 to 6 minutes.

2. Add the onion, carrots, and garlic, and season with the salt and pepper. Cook until the onion has softened, 3 to 5 minutes.

3. Stir in the tomato paste, then the tomatoes. Bring to a boil, and remove from the heat.

4. Spoon 2 cups of the meat mixture into the bottom of the slow cooker. Layer 3 noodles (breaking them, as needed, to fit), 2 cups meat mixture, and ½ cup mozzarella. Repeat, with two more layers. Refrigerate the remaining ½ cup mozzarella for topping.

5. Cover and cook on low for 4 to 6 hours. Sprinkle the lasagna with the remaining ½ cup mozzarella. Cover and cook until the cheese has melted, about 10 minutes.

6. Serve hot.

Spanish Meatballs

SERVES 8

Everyone loves meatballs, and these are especially delicious: Hot smoked paprika adds a burst of flavor, as does the ground pork. Of course, slow cooking guarantees that these meatballs are extra juicy and tender. If you don't want to use ground pork, these are just as tasty with ground turkey or beef, or even a blend. Serve these over cooked pasta or polenta, nice and hot.

2 POUNDS GROUND PORK

1 MEDIUM YELLOW ONION, FINELY CHOPPED

1½ TEASPOONS GROUND CUMIN

1½ TEASPOONS HOT SMOKED PAPRIKA

5 TABLESPOONS PLAIN DRIED BREAD CRUMBS

2 LARGE EGGS, LIGHTLY BEATEN

3 TABLESPOONS CHOPPED FRESH PARSLEY

COARSE SEA SALT

BLACK PEPPER

3 TABLESPOONS EXTRA-VIRGIN OLIVE OIL

ONE 28-OUNCE CAN DICED TOMATOES, WITH THE JUICE

RUSTIC BREAD, FOR SERVING (OPTIONAL)

1. In a large bowl, combine the pork, ¼ cup of the onion, cumin, ½ teaspoon of the paprika, bread crumbs, eggs, and parsley. Season with the salt and pepper. Mix thoroughly to combine.

2. Roll the meat mixture into 25 meatballs (each about 1½ inches), and put on a plate.

3. In a large nonstick skillet, heat 1½ tablespoons of the olive oil over medium-high heat. In two batches, brown the meatballs on all sides, 8 minutes per batch. Transfer the browned meatballs to the slow cooker.

4. Add the remaining onion to the skillet, and cook until fragrant, stirring often, about 2 minutes. Transfer the onion to the slow cooker, sprinkle in the remaining 1 teaspoon paprika, and add the tomatoes. Season with salt and pepper.

5. Cover and cook on low until the meatballs are tender, 5 hours. Serve with slices of rustic bread, if desired.

Ragout of Veal

The term ragout, *which means a main dish stew, derives from the French* ragoûter, *which means "to revive the taste." Very similar in both etymological origin and gastronomical composition to the Italian* ragù, *both are often used to dress pasta and other starches. Since ragouts are cooked over low heat, this is a slow cooker natural.*

ONE 2½-POUND BONELESS VEAL TIP ROUND ROAST, TRIMMED

1½ TEASPOONS PAPRIKA

¾ TEASPOON BLACK PEPPER

½ TEASPOON SEA SALT

1 TABLESPOON OLIVE OIL

½ CUP DRY WHITE WINE

3 LARGE LEEKS, SLICED

3 CLOVES GARLIC, MINCED

⅓ CUP ALL-PURPOSE FLOUR

ONE 14-OUNCE CAN CHICKEN STOCK

3 LARGE CARROTS, CUT INTO ½-INCH SLICES

5 FRESH THYME SPRIGS

1 BAY LEAF

8 CUPS HOT COOKED FETTUCCINE (ABOUT 16 OUNCES UNCOOKED PASTA)

2 TABLESPOONS CHOPPED FRESH FLAT-LEAF PARSLEY

1. Cut the veal into 1-inch cubes and place in a large bowl. Sprinkle the paprika, pepper, and salt over the veal.

2. Heat a large skillet over medium-high heat. Add 1 teaspoon of the olive oil and swirl to coat the pan. Add one-half of the veal, and sauté 4 minutes or until browned. Place the browned veal in the slow cooker. Repeat, with 1 teaspoon of the oil and the remaining one-half of the veal.

3. Add the wine to the skillet and cook 1 minute, scraping pan to loosen browned bits. Pour over the veal in the slow cooker.

continued ▶

Ragout of Veal *continued* ▶

4. To the skillet over medium-high heat, add the remaining 1 teaspoon oil to pan and swirl to coat. Add the leeks and garlic and sauté for 3 minutes. Spoon the leek mixture over the veal in the slow cooker.

5. Place the flour in a small bowl, and gradually add the stock, stirring until well blended. Pour the broth mixture into the slow cooker.

6. Add the carrots, thyme sprigs, and bay leaf, and stir.

7. Cover and cook on low for 3 to 5 hours, or until the veal is tender.

8. Discard the thyme sprigs and bay leaf. Serve the veal and vegetables over the hot fettucine, sprinkled with parsley.

Beef Daube Provençal

SERVES 8

Daube is a classic, thick stew originating in Provence, a region in Southern France. It is typically made with inexpensive cuts of beef braised in red wine and spiced with herbes de Provence, a traditional regional spice blend. "Slow cooking" is the watchword for a daube, and cooking in stages with cooling in between is the traditional way of making this dish. It is a natural for your slow cooker.

2 POUNDS BONELESS CHUCK ROAST, TRIMMED, AND CUT INTO CHUNKS

1 TABLESPOON EXTRA-VIRGIN OLIVE OIL

6 CLOVES GARLIC, MINCED

½ CUP BOILING WATER

½ OUNCE DRIED PORCINI MUSHROOMS

¼ TEASPOON SEA SALT PLUS ½ TEASPOON

NONSTICK COOKING OIL SPRAY

½ CUP RED WINE

¼ CUP BEEF STOCK

⅓ CUP PITTED NIÇOISE OLIVES

½ TEASPOON BLACK PEPPER

2 LARGE CARROTS, THINLY SLICED

1 LARGE YELLOW ONION, CHOPPED

1 CELERY STALK, THINLY SLICED

ONE 15-OUNCE CAN WHOLE TOMATOES, DRAINED AND CRUSHED

1 TEASPOON WHOLE BLACK PEPPERCORNS

3 FRESH FLAT-LEAF PARSLEY SPRIGS

3 FRESH THYME SPRIGS

1 BAY LEAF

ONE 1-INCH STRIP ORANGE RIND

1 TABLESPOON WATER

1 TEASPOON CORNSTARCH

1½ TABLESPOONS CHOPPED FRESH FLAT-LEAF PARSLEY LEAVES

1½ TEASPOONS CHOPPED FRESH THYME LEAVES

continued ▶

Beef Daube Provençal *continued* ▶

1. Combine the beef chunks, olive oil, and garlic in large resealable plastic bag. Seal and marinate at room temperature 30 minutes, turning the bag occasionally. Pour out into a medium bowl.

2. Combine ½ cup boiling water and the mushrooms in a small bowl. Cover and let stand 30 minutes. Drain through a sieve over a bowl, reserving the mushrooms and ¼ cup of the soaking liquid. Chop the mushrooms.

3. Coat a large skillet with cooking oil spray. Heat over medium-high heat.

4. Sprinkle the beef mixture with ¼ teaspoon of the salt. Add one-half of the beef mixture to the pan and sauté 5 minutes, turning to brown on all sides. Place the browned beef mixture in the slow cooker. Repeat with the remaining half of the beef mixture.

5. Add the wine and stock to the skillet. Bring to a boil, scraping the pan with a wooden spoon to loosen the flavorful browned bits. Pour the wine mixture into the slow cooker.

6. Add the mushrooms, reserved ¼ cup soaking liquid, remaining ½ teaspoon salt, olives, pepper, carrots, onion, celery, and tomatoes to the slow cooker.

7. Place the peppercorns, parsley sprigs, thyme sprigs, bay leaf, and orange rind on a square, double layer of cheesecloth. Gather the corners of the cheesecloth together and secure with kitchen twine. Add the herb bundle to the slow cooker.

8. Cover and cook on low for 6 hours or until the beef and vegetables are tender. Discard the cheesecloth bundle.

9. Whisk the 1 tablespoon water with the cornstarch in a small bowl, stirring until smooth. Add the cornstarch mixture to the slow cooker and cook for 20 minutes or until slightly thick, stirring occasionally.

10. Serve hot, sprinkled with the chopped parsley and chopped thyme.

Osso Buco in Bianco with Gremolata

SERVES 8

Ossobuco means "bone with a hole" in Italian, and it refers to the central marrow bone hole of the cross-cut veal shank that is the subject of the dish. The more traditional version of the dish, osso buco in bianco, is the one represented in this recipe and is flavored with gremolata— a condiment made of garlic, lemon zest, and parsley.

⅔ CUP ALL-PURPOSE FLOUR

¾ TEASPOON BLACK PEPPER

½ TEASPOON SEA SALT

6 VEAL SHANKS, TRIMMED

2 TEASPOONS BUTTER

2 TEASPOONS OLIVE OIL

2 LARGE RED ONIONS, COARSELY CHOPPED

2 LARGE STALKS CELERY, CHOPPED

6 CLOVES GARLIC, MINCED

4 CUPS BEEF STOCK

2 CUPS DRY WHITE WINE

1 TABLESPOON CHOPPED FRESH ROSEMARY LEAVES

1 TABLESPOON ANCHOVY PASTE

GREMOLATA

½ CUP CHOPPED FRESH FLAT-LEAF PARSLEY

1 TABLESPOON LEMON ZEST

2 CLOVES GARLIC, MINCED

8 CUPS HOT COOKED PAPPARDELLE PASTA (ABOUT 1 POUND UNCOOKED WIDE RIBBON PASTA), FOR SERVING

1. Combine the flour, ¼ teaspoon of the pepper, and ¼ teaspoon of the salt in a shallow dish. Dredge the veal shanks in the flour mixture.

continued ▶

Osso Buco in Bianco with Gremolata *continued* ▶

2. Heat 1 teaspoon of the butter and 1 teaspoon of the olive oil in a large skillet over medium heat. Add one-half of the veal and cook for 6 minutes, browning on both sides. Place the browned veal in the slow cooker. Repeat, with the remaining butter, oil, and veal.

3. Add the onions and celery to the skillet, and sauté 5 minutes over medium-high heat or until tender. Add the garlic and sauté 1 minute.

4. Stir in the stock, wine, rosemary, and anchovy paste, scraping the bottom of the pan with a wooden spoon to loosen the flavorful browned bits. Bring to a boil and cook 4 minutes. Pour over the veal.

5. Cover and cook on low for 9 hours or until done.

6. Sprinkle the veal with the remaining ½ teaspoon pepper and ¼ teaspoon salt. Remove the veal to a warm platter.

7. To make the gremolata: Combine the parsley, lemon zest, and garlic in a small bowl and stir to combine.

8. To serve, place 1 cup of the pasta in each of eight pasta bowls. Top with ⅔ cup veal and ½ cup broth mixture. (Reserve remaining broth mixture for another use.) Sprinkle each serving with 1 tablespoon of the gremolata.

Moroccan Meatballs in Spicy Tomato Sauce

SERVES 6

Seasoned meatballs simmer in an aromatic tomato sauce for a Mediterranean-style dinner. Use kitchen shears or two sharp knives to coarsely chop the tomatoes while they are still in the can. You can shape the meatballs in advance and store them in the freezer (then thaw) to save time. The rest of the recipe is best prepared and cooked the same day.

MOROCCAN MEATBALLS

½ CUP BREAD CRUMBS

¼ CUP DRIED CURRANTS

½ YELLOW ONION, FINELY CHOPPED

½ TEASPOON SEA SALT

½ TEASPOON GROUND CUMIN

½ TEASPOON DRIED OREGANO

¼ TEASPOON GROUND CINNAMON

1½ POUNDS LEAN GROUND BEEF

1 LARGE EGG WHITE

SPICY TOMATO SAUCE

¼ CUP TOMATO PASTE

1 TEASPOON FENNEL SEEDS

1 TEASPOON ORANGE ZEST

½ TEASPOON GROUND CUMIN

¼ TEASPOON GROUND CINNAMON

¼ TEASPOON SEA SALT

¼ TEASPOON GROUND RED PEPPER

ONE 28-OUNCE CAN WHOLE TOMATOES, COARSELY CHOPPED, WITH THE JUICE

3 CUPS HOT COOKED COUSCOUS, FOR SERVING

2 TABLESPOONS FRESH CHOPPED PARSLEY (OPTIONAL), FOR SERVING

continued ▶

Moroccan Meatballs in Spicy Tomato Sauce *continued* ▶

To prepare the meatballs:

1. Combine the bread crumbs, currants, onion, salt, cumin, oregano, cinnamon, beef, and egg white in a medium bowl. Shape the meat mixture into 30 meatballs and place on a plate.

2. Heat a large nonstick skillet over medium-high heat. Add half of the meatballs to the pan and cook for 3 minutes or until browned, turning frequently. Place the browned meatballs in the slow cooker. Repeat, with the remaining 15 meatballs.

To prepare the sauce:

1. Combine the tomato paste, fennel seeds, orange zest, cumin, cinnamon, salt, red pepper, and tomatoes in a medium bowl. Add to the slow cooker and stir gently to coat the meatballs with sauce.

2. Cover and cook on low for 6 hours.

3. Serve over the couscous. Garnish with parsley, if desired.

Beef Bourguignon with Egg Noodles

Beef bourguignon originates from the Bourgogne region of France (called Burgundy in English). It features beef braised in red wine, traditionally red burgundy, although a Chianti or Zinfandel will work just as well. Beef stock, garlic, onions, and herbs also lend this dish its flavor.

2 POUNDS LEAN BEEF STEW MEAT

6 TABLESPOONS ALL-PURPOSE FLOUR

2 LARGE CARROTS CUT INTO 1-INCH SLICES

16 OUNCES PEARL ONIONS, PEELED FRESH OR FROZEN, THAWED

8 OUNCES MUSHROOMS, STEMS REMOVED

2 GARLIC CLOVES, MINCED

¾ CUP BEEF STOCK

½ CUP DRY RED WINE

¼ CUP TOMATO PASTE

1½ TEASPOONS SEA SALT

½ TEASPOON DRIED ROSEMARY

¼ TEASPOON DRIED THYME

½ TEASPOON BLACK PEPPER

8 OUNCES UNCOOKED EGG NOODLES

¼ CUP CHOPPED FRESH THYME LEAVES

1. Place the beef in a medium bowl, sprinkle with the flour, and toss well to coat.

2. Place the beef mixture, carrots, onions, mushrooms, and garlic in the slow cooker.

3. Combine the stock, wine, tomato paste, salt, rosemary, thyme, and black pepper in a small bowl. Stir into the beef mixture.

4. Cover and cook on low for 8 hours.

5. Cook the noodles according to package directions, omitting any salt.

6. Serve the beef mixture over the noodles, sprinkled with the thyme.

Beef Ragù

SERVES 6

Unlike the familiar jarred spaghetti sauces in grocery stores, traditional ragù is typically a sauce of braised meat that may be flavored with tomato—not tomato sauce with meat in it. In parts of Southern Italy, especially Campania, substantial quantities of large, whole cuts of beef and pork are often the basis for ragùs. These larger cuts, like in this recipe, are slowly braised over time and then served as a separate course without pasta.

1 MEDIUM YELLOW ONION, DICED SMALL

3 CLOVES GARLIC, MINCED

6 TABLESPOONS TOMATO PASTE

3 TABLESPOONS CHOPPED FRESH OREGANO LEAVES (OR 3 TEASPOONS DRIED OREGANO)

ONE 4-POUND BEEF CHUCK ROAST, HALVED

COARSE SEA SALT

BLACK PEPPER

2 CUPS BEEF STOCK

2 TABLESPOONS RED WINE VINEGAR

1. Combine the onion, garlic, tomato paste, and oregano in the slow cooker.

2. Season the roast halves with salt and pepper and place on top of the onion mixture in the slow cooker. Add the beef stock.

3. Cover and cook until meat is tender and can easily be pulled apart with a fork, on high for 4½ hours, or on low for 9 hours. Let cool 10 minutes.

4. Shred the meat while it is still in the slow cooker using two forks. Stir the vinegar into the sauce. Serve hot, over pasta.

Beef Brisket with Onions

SERVES 6

Slow cooking leads to fall-apart, tender brisket you'll enjoy serving, along with enjoying the compliments on your cooking. A whole brisket comprises a first and second cut; for this recipe, if possible, opt for the leaner first cut, also called the "flat cut." The fat layer should be trimmed down to ¼ inch, which is plenty for keeping the meat moist as it cooks.

1 LARGE YELLOW ONION, THINLY SLICED

2 GARLIC CLOVES, SMASHED AND PEELED

1 FIRST CUT OF BEEF BRISKET (4 POUNDS), TRIMMED OF EXCESS FAT

COARSE SEA SALT

BLACK PEPPER

2 CUPS CHICKEN BROTH

2 TABLESPOONS CHOPPED FRESH PARSLEY LEAVES, FOR SERVING

1. Combine the onion and garlic in the slow cooker.

2. Season the brisket with salt and pepper, and place, fat-side up, in the slow cooker.

3. Add the broth to the slow cooker. Cover and cook until the brisket is fork-tender, on high for about 6 hours.

4. Remove the brisket to a cutting board and thinly slice across the grain.

5. Serve with the onion and some cooking liquid, sprinkled with parsley.

Italian Pot Roast

SERVES 8

The subtle difference between this dish and an American-style pot roast is barely noticeable. The main difference is the presence of tomatoes. But in any event, this recipe produces a pot roast that is homey and delicious.

ONE 3-POUND BEEF CHUCK ROAST, TRIMMED AND HALVED CROSSWISE

4 CLOVES GARLIC, HALVED LENGTHWISE

1½ TEASPOONS COARSE SEA SALT

1 TEASPOON BLACK PEPPER

1 TABLESPOON OLIVE OIL

1 LARGE YELLOW ONION, CUT INTO 8 WEDGES

1¼ POUNDS SMALL WHITE POTATOES

ONE 28-OUNCE CAN WHOLE TOMATOES IN PURÉE

1 TABLESPOON CHOPPED FRESH ROSEMARY LEAVES (OR 1 TEASPOON DRIED AND
CRUMBLED ROSEMARY)

1. With a sharp paring knife, cut four slits in each of the beef roast halves, and stuff the slits with one-half of the garlic halves. Generously season the beef with the salt and pepper.

2. In a large skillet, heat the olive oil over medium-high heat, swirling to coat the bottom of the pan. Cook the beef until browned on all sides, about 5 minutes.

3. Combine the beef, onion, potatoes, tomatoes, rosemary, and the remaining garlic in the slow cooker.

4. Cover and cook until the meat is fork-tender, on high for about 6 hours.

5. Transfer the meat to a cutting board. Thinly slice, and discard any fat or gristle.

6. Skim the fat from the top of the sauce in the slow cooker.

7. Serve hot, dividing the beef and vegetables among the eight bowls, and generously spooning the sauce over the top.

CHAPTER NINE

Desserts

Although you might not think of your slow cooker when you think of dessert, this chapter is going to change that. These amazing recipes will allow you to create delectable, sweet desserts in no time at all. You'll love the way cakes and cheesecakes come out in your slow cooker: moist, smooth, and with excellent texture. Puddings and custards have plenty of time to cook and set perfectly in the slow cooker. And there's no better place to stew or roast fruit.

Red Wine Poached Pears

Spiced Fruit Compote

Stuffed Spiced Apples

Mixed Berry Clafoutis

Bananas Foster

Tiramisu Bread Pudding

Rum Raisin Arborio Pudding

Chocolate Hazelnut Bread Pudding

Natillas de Avellanas (Spanish Hazelnut Brandy Custard)

Sour Cream Amaretti Cheesecake

Blood Orange Upside-Down Cake

Moroccan Golden Saffron Cake

Red Wine Poached Pears

SERVES 6

These poached pears are strikingly beautiful, yet simple to prepare. If you're looking for a delicious dessert that won't fail to impress, this is the one.

6 PEARS, PEELED, CORED, AND HALVED
ONE 750 ML BOTTLE RED WINE
1 CUP GRANULATED SUGAR
1 TEASPOON VANILLA
1 CINNAMON STICK
2 STAR ANISE
1 CUP WHIPPING CREAM
1 TABLESPOON CONFECTIONERS' SUGAR

1. Place pear halves in the slow cooker.

2. Add the wine to the slow cooker.

3. Stir the sugar into the slow cooker, trying to keep the pear halves undisturbed.

4. Add the vanilla, cinnamon stick, and star anise to the slow cooker.

5. Cover and cook on low for 5 hours or on high for 2 hours.

6. About 10 minutes before the cooking time has elapsed, whip the cream with the confectioners' sugar.

7. Serve the pears warm in bowls with a dollop of sweetened whipped cream.

Spiced Fruit Compote

SERVES 10 TO 12

This dessert is wonderfully simple and can go with anything from ice cream to cookies or cake. It also is delicious just plain.

3 MEDIUM-SIZE PEARS, PEELED, CORED, AND CUBED
ONE 16-OUNCE CAN PINEAPPLE, IN CUBES OR CHUNKS, WITH THE JUICE
1 CUP QUARTERED DRIED APRICOTS
3 TABLESPOONS FROZEN ORANGE JUICE CONCENTRATE
2 TABLESPOONS PACKED LIGHT BROWN SUGAR
1 TABLESPOON QUICK-COOKING TAPIOCA
1 TEASPOON GRATED PEELED FRESH GINGER (OR ½ TEASPOON DRIED GROUND GINGER)
2 CUPS PITTED DARK, SWEET CHERRIES
1 CUP TOASTED SHREDDED UNSWEETENED COCONUT
1 CUP CHOPPED AND TOASTED MACADAMIA NUTS OR PECANS

1. In the slow cooker, combine the pears, pineapple and juice, apricots, orange juice concentrate, brown sugar, tapioca, and ginger.

2. Cover and cook on low for 6 to 8 hours or on high for 3 to 4 hours. At 30 minutes before the cooking time ends, stir in the cherries.

3. Serve warm, topped with the coconut and nuts.

Stuffed Spiced Apples

SERVES 4

This simple, tasty dessert makes the most of fresh apples, dried fruits, and nuts. Baked, stuffed apples are also an American comfort dish, so these flavors will taste familiar to you.

4 MEDIUM-SIZED TART COOKING APPLES (LIKE GRANNY SMITH OR BRAEBURN)
⅓ CUP FINELY CHOPPED DRIED FIGS OR RAISINS
½ CUP FINELY CHOPPED WALNUTS
¼ CUP PACKED LIGHT BROWN SUGAR
½ TEASPOON APPLE PIE SPICE OR CINNAMON
¼ CUP APPLE JUICE
1 TABLESPOON BUTTER, CUT INTO 4 PIECES

1. Core the apples. Cut a strip of peel from the top of each apple. Place the apples upright in the slow cooker.

2. In a small bowl, combine figs, walnuts, brown sugar, and apple pie spice. Spoon the mixture into the center of the apples, patting in with a knife or a narrow metal spatula.

3. Pour the apple juice around the apples in the slow cooker.

4. Top each apple with a piece of butter.

5. Cover and cook on low for 4 to 5 hours or on high for 2 to 2½ hours until very tender.

6. Serve warm, with some of the cooking liquid spooned over the apples.

Mixed Berry Clafoutis

SERVES 6

Clafoutis is a French baked dessert of fruit, typically black cherries. The fruit is arranged in a buttered dish, covered with a thick batter, and baked. The clafoutis is often dusted with confectioners' sugar and served warm, often with cream. It is similar to an American cobbler.

1 CUP ALL-PURPOSE FLOUR

1¾ CUPS GRANULATED SUGAR

1 TEASPOON BAKING POWDER

¼ TEASPOON SALT

¼ TEASPOON GROUND CINNAMON

¼ TEASPOON GROUND NUTMEG

2 EGGS, LIGHTLY BEATEN

3 TEASPOONS OLIVE OIL (*NOT* EXTRA-VIRGIN)

2 TABLESPOONS MILK

2 CUPS FRESH BLUEBERRIES

2 CUPS FRESH RASPBERRIES

2 CUPS FRESH BLACKBERRIES

1 CUP WATER

3 TABLESPOONS UNCOOKED QUICK-COOKING TAPIOCA

WHIPPED CREAM, FOR SERVING

1. In a medium bowl, stir together the flour, ¾ cup of the sugar, baking powder, salt, cinnamon, and nutmeg.

2. In a small bowl, whisk together the eggs, olive oil, and milk.

3. Add the egg mixture to the flour mixture and stir to combine, just until moistened. Set aside.

4. In a large heavy saucepan over medium heat, combine the blueberries, raspberries, blackberries, the remaining 1 cup sugar, the water, and the tapioca. Bring to a boil.

5. Pour the hot fruit mixture into the slow cooker. Immediately spoon the batter over the fruit mixture.

continued ▶

Mixed Berry Clafoutis *continued* ▶

6. Cover and cook on high for 1¾ to 2 hours or until a toothpick inserted into the center of the cake topper comes out clean.

7. Remove the crock from the cooker, if possible, or uncover and turn off the cooker. Let stand, uncovered, for 1 hour to cool slightly.

8. To serve, spoon the warm clafoutis into dessert dishes and top with the whipped cream.

Bananas Foster

SERVES 8

This classic dessert created in the French Quarter of New Orleans exemplifies basic Mediterranean cooking style. The use of fresh fruit and simple ingredients, for example, with a touch of spice, affords this dish not only unbeatable flavor, but also style and sophistication.

NONSTICK COOKING OIL SPRAY
1 CUP DARK BROWN SUGAR
¼ CUP BUTTER
¼ CUP DARK RUM
¼ CUP BANANA LIQUEUR
½ TEASPOON GROUND CINNAMON
4 RIPE BANANAS, CUT IN HALF LENGTHWISE, THEN HALVED CROSSWISE
2 CUPS VANILLA ICE CREAM, FOR SERVING

1. Coat the interior of the slow cooker crock with nonstick cooking oil spray.

2. Combine the brown sugar, butter, rum, and banana liqueur in the slow cooker.

3. Cover and cook on low for 1 hour. Stir the sauce with a whisk until smooth.

4. Add the cinnamon and bananas to the sauce, and spoon the sauce over to coat. Cover and cook on low for 15 minutes.

5. Serve hot with a scoop of ice cream.

Tiramisu Bread Pudding

SERVES 10

This bread pudding is wonderfully moist. Flavored with coffee and Kahlúa, with a rich mascarpone sauce added, this dessert the perfect vehicle for each of the classic flavors of tiramisu.

½ CUP WATER

⅓ CUP GRANULATED SUGAR

1½ TABLESPOONS INSTANT ESPRESSO GRANULES

2 TABLESPOONS COFFEE-FLAVORED LIQUEUR (LIKE KAHLÚA)

2 CUPS WHOLE MILK

2 LARGE EGGS, LIGHTLY BEATEN

8 OUNCES FRENCH BREAD, CUT INTO 1-INCH CUBES (ABOUT 8 CUPS)

NONSTICK COOKING OIL SPRAY

⅓ CUP MASCARPONE CHEESE

1 TEASPOON VANILLA EXTRACT

2 TEASPOONS UNSWEETENED COCOA POWDER

1. Combine the water, sugar, and espresso granules in a small saucepan over medium-hugh heat. Bring to a boil, and boil 1 minute, stirring occasionally. Remove from the heat, and stir in the liqueur.

2. Combine 1¾ cups of the milk and the eggs in a large bowl, stirring with a whisk. Whisk in the espresso mixture. Add the bread cubes, and stir to coat.

3. Coat a 2½-quart round baking dish with nonstick cooking oil spray. Pour the bread mixture into the baking dish. Place the dish in slow cooker. Cover and cook on low for 2 hours or until set. Remove from the slow cooker and let cool. Refrigerate until chilled, about 3 hours.

4. Combine the remaining ¼ cup milk, mascarpone cheese, and vanilla in a small bowl, and stir with a whisk until smooth. To serve, top the chilled bread pudding with the mascarpone sauce, and sprinkle with some of the cocoa.

Rum Raisin Arborio Pudding

Arborio rice is generally used for risotto because it gives the dish such a creamy texture. For this reason, it makes wonderful rice pudding. Soaking the raisins in rum allows them to plump up and soak in the rum before they even become part of the pudding. Evaporated milk is best in slow cooker recipes like this one because it doesn't curdle.

½ CUP RAISINS

¼ CUP DARK RUM

ONE 12-OUNCE CAN EVAPORATED MILK

1½ CUPS WATER

⅓ CUP GRANULATED SUGAR

¾ CUP ARBORIO RICE

¼ TEASPOON SALT

¼ TEASPOON GROUND NUTMEG

1. Combine the raisins and rum in a small bowl. Cover and set aside.

2. Combine the evaporated milk and 1½ cups water in a heavy medium saucepan. Bring to a simmer over medium heat. Add the sugar, stirring to dissolve. Remove from the heat.

3. Pour the milk mixture into the slow cooker. Stir in the rice and salt.

4. Cover and cook on low for 4 hours, stirring after 1 hour and again after 3 hours. The pudding is finished when it is just set in the center.

5. Drain the raisins, and stir them into the pudding. Stir in the nutmeg. Let stand, uncovered, 10 minutes. Serve warm, or chill in the fridge for about 3 hours in dessert cups.

Chocolate Hazelnut Bread Pudding

SERVES 8 TO 10

The addition of chocolate chips gives this recipe an additional boost alongside the rich, creamy Nutella. Once cooked, the chocolate chips melt and become gooey. If you cannot find challah bread, use other firm, high-quality sandwich bread in its place. If your bread is stale, that's better still, because you can skip toasting the bread.

NONSTICK COOKING OIL SPRAY

14 OUNCES CHALLAH BREAD, CUT INTO 1-INCH CUBES (ABOUT 12 CUPS)

½ CUP SEMISWEET CHOCOLATE CHIPS

2 CUPS HEAVY CREAM

2 CUPS WHOLE MILK

9 LARGE EGG YOLKS, ROOM TEMPERATURE

1 CUP CHOCOLATE HAZELNUT SPREAD (LIKE NUTELLA)

¾ CUP GRANULATED SUGAR PLUS 1 TABLESPOON

4 TEASPOONS VANILLA EXTRACT

¾ TEASPOON SALT

2 TABLESPOONS LIGHT BROWN SUGAR

1. Line the slow cooker with aluminum foil; then coat with nonstick cooking oil spray.

2. Adjust the oven rack to the middle position and preheat the oven to 225°F.

3. Spread the bread cubes over a baking sheet and bake, shaking the pan occasionally, until dry and crisp, about 40 minutes. Let the bread cool for 5 minutes; then transfer it to very large bowl.

4. Mix the chocolate chips into the dried bread cubes, and transfer to the prepared slow cooker.

5. Whisk the cream, milk, egg yolks, chocolate hazelnut spread, ¾ cup of the sugar, vanilla, and salt together in a large bowl; then pour the mixture evenly over the bread cubes in the slow cooker. Press gently on the bread to submerge.

6. Mix the remaining 1 tablespoon granulated sugar with the brown sugar in a small bowl, then sprinkle it over the top of the bread cube mixture.

7. Cover and cook on low until the center is set, about 4 hours.

8. Let cool for 30 minutes. You can remove the bread pudding from the slow cooker by pulling it up by the foil edges, then placing it in a large shallow bowl. Serve warm or chilled.

Natillas de Avellanas (Spanish Hazelnut Brandy Custard)

SERVES 4

Spanish custard, called natillas, *is a smooth, rich custard flavored with brandy and hazelnuts. Best eaten warm, this is one of the foods that remind many Spanish people fondly of their childhood days. The use of evaporated milk in the recipe helps prevent curdling.*

12 OUNCES EVAPORATED MILK

½ CUP MILK

1 TEASPOON VANILLA BEAN PASTE

1 EGG, LIGHTLY BEATEN

2 EGG YOLKS

⅓ CUP SUGAR

2 OUNCES BLANCHED HAZELNUTS, GROUND

2 TO 3 OUNCES BRANDY

1. Combine the evaporated milk and the milk in a medium heavy saucepan over medium heat. Bring to a simmer and cook about 4 minutes. Remove from the heat, add the vanilla bean paste, and stir with a whisk until blended.

2. Combine the egg, egg yolks, and sugar in a medium bowl. Whisk until blended.

3. Gradually add the hot milk to egg mixture, whisking vigorously.

4. Pour the egg mixture through a sieve into a medium bowl. Stir in the hazelnuts and brandy.

5. Place four metal canning jar bands in the bottom of the slow cooker.

6. Ladle the egg mixture evenly into four 8-ounce ramekins. Cover the ramekins with foil.

7. Set the ramekins on the jar bands, making sure they do not touch each other or the sides of the slow cooker. Carefully pour hot water into the slow cooker to a depth of 1 inch up sides of the ramekins.

8. Cover and cook on high for 1 hour and 45 minutes or until a knife inserted in center of the custards comes out clean. Remove the ramekins from slow cooker, and cool on a wire rack.

9. Serve warm or chilled.

Sour Cream Amaretti Cheesecake

SERVES 6

Cheesecake is wonderful cooked in a slow cooker, because the cooker steams it throughout the cooking process. This recipe is particularly delicious and rich, thanks to the presence of sour cream and amaretti cookies in place of the standard graham crackers. You'll need a slow cooker that has a steaming rack and will accommodate a 6-inch springform pan.

¾ CUP AMARETTI COOKIE CRUMBS (AROUND 3 OUNCES OR 20 COOKIES, CRUSHED)

2½ TABLESPOONS UNSALTED BUTTER, MELTED

½ TEASPOON SALT

¼ TEASPOON GROUND CINNAMON

⅔ CUP GRANULATED SUGAR, PLUS 1 TABLESPOON

12 OUNCES CREAM CHEESE (ONE 8-OUNCE PACKAGE PLUS ONE 4-OUNCE PACKAGE),
    AT ROOM TEMPERATURE

1 TABLESPOON ALL-PURPOSE FLOUR

2 LARGE EGGS

1 TEASPOON ALMOND EXTRACT

1 CUP SOUR CREAM

1. In a medium bowl, mix the cookie crumbs, melted butter, ¼ teaspoon of the salt, cinnamon, and 1 tablespoon sugar. Press the crumb mixture into a 6-inch springform pan, covering the bottom of pan and going about 1 inch up the side of the pan to form a crust.

2. With an electric mixer in a medium bowl, combine the cream cheese, flour, remaining ⅔ cup sugar, and remaining ¼ teaspoon salt. Beat at medium-high until smooth.

3. Scrape down the sides of bowl. Add the eggs and the almond extract. Beat until blended.

4. Add the sour cream and beat until smooth.

5. Pour the batter over the cookie crumb crust in the springform pan.

continued ▶

Sour Cream Amaretti Cheesecake *continued* ▶

6. Fill the slow cooker with ½ inch water and place the rack in the bottom, making sure the top of the rack is above the water. Set the springform pan with the cheesecake in it on the rack. Cover the slow cooker with a triple layer of paper towels, and then cover with the lid. Cook on high for 2 hours without opening the slow cooker even once.

7. Turn off the heat and let stand until cooker has cooled, again without opening lid, at least 1 additional hour.

8. Remove the cheesecake and chill for about 3 hours before serving in wedges.

Blood Orange Upside-Down Cake

SERVES 6 TO 8

This spectacular dessert is as delicious as it is beautiful. Blood oranges are wonderfully sweet as well as visually striking, but if you can't find them, you can use standard oranges. Use a knife to peel the oranges and be sure to remove all of the bitter white pith.

ORANGE LAYER

5 TABLESPOONS UNSALTED BUTTER, CUT INTO SMALL PIECES, PLUS MORE FOR SLOW
    COOKER CROCK

¾ CUP FIRMLY PACKED DARK BROWN SUGAR

3 TABLESPOONS DARK RUM

2 POUNDS BLOOD ORANGES (ABOUT 6), SLICED, PEELED, WITH ALL OF THE BITTER WHITE
    PITH REMOVED

½ TEASPOON GROUND CARDAMOM

CAKE

¾ CUPS CAKE FLOUR

¾ TEASPOONS BAKING POWDER

½ TEASPOON GROUND CINNAMON

¼ TEASPOON GROUND NUTMEG

¼ TEASPOON SALT

4 TABLESPOONS UNSALTED BUTTER, AT ROOM TEMPERATURE

⅔ CUP GRANULATED SUGAR

1 EGG, AT ROOM TEMPERATURE

1 EGG YOLK, AT ROOM TEMPERATURE

2 TABLESPOONS WHOLE MILK, AT ROOM TEMPERATURE

2 CUPS VANILLA ICE CREAM, FOR SERVING (OPTIONAL)

continued ▶

Blood Orange Upside-Down Cake *continued* ▶

To make the orange layer:

1. Butter the inside of the slow cooker crock, line completely with foil, and then butter the foil.

2. Sprinkle the butter, brown sugar, and rum over the foil on the bottom of the slow cooker. Cover that with the orange slices in a slightly overlapping pattern, and sprinkle with the cardamom. Press the oranges into the sugar.

To make the cake:

1. Sift the flour, baking powder, cinnamon, nutmeg, and salt into a large bowl. Whisk gently to combine evenly.

2. In a medium bowl, slowly beat the butter and sugar with an electric mixer until just blended. Raise the speed to high and beat until light and fluffy, scraping down the sides of the bowl occasionally, about 10 minutes.

3. Beat the egg and then the egg yolk into the butter-sugar mixture, allowing each to be fully incorporated before adding the next.

4. While mixing slowly, add the flour mixture to the butter-sugar mixture in three parts, alternating with the milk in two parts, beginning and ending with the flour. Mix briefly at medium speed to make a smooth batter.

5. Pour the batter over the oranges in the slow cooker and smooth with a spatula to even it out.

6. Lay a doubled length of paper towel from end to end over the top of the slow cooker, to line the lid and create a tighter seal.

7. Cover the cake tightly with the lid and cook on high until the cake begins to brown slightly on the sides and springs back when touched in the middle, about 3½ hours. Turn off the slow cooker and let the cake set, uncovered, about 20 minutes more.

8. Using the foil, lift the cake from the slow cooker and set on the counter to cool, about 30 minutes more. Fold back the foil, and carefully invert the cake onto a platter so the caramelized oranges are visible on top.

9. Slice or spoon the cake into bowls, and serve with ice cream, if desired.

Moroccan Golden Saffron Cake

SERVES 10

This cake is truly a special treat. You can often find rosewater for baking in the international aisle of your supermarket, and you can also find it online. If you cannot find rosewater, simply use 3 tablespoons of vanilla extract in the cake batter, with an extra ½ teaspoon vanilla for the vanilla syrup.

1 TEASPOON SAFFRON THREADS, CRUSHED IN YOUR PALM

1 TABLESPOON BUTTER, AT ROOM TEMPERATURE

2 TABLESPOONS WHOLE MILK

NONSTICK COOKING OIL SPRAY

1½ CUPS CAKE FLOUR

1 TEASPOON BAKING POWDER

½ TEASPOON BAKING SODA

½ TEASPOON SALT

3 EGGS

1¾ CUPS GRANULATED SUGAR

2 TABLESPOONS ROSEWATER

1½ TEASPOONS VANILLA

1 CUP CHOPPED PITTED DATES

1 CUP DICED DRIED APRICOTS

2 CUPS COARSELY CHOPPED TOASTED WALNUTS

¾ CUP WATER

1 TABLESPOON FINELY CHOPPED PISTACHIO NUTS

1. Put the saffron threads, butter, and 2 tablespoons of the milk in a small saucepan over medium-high heat. Bring to a simmer while contantly stirring, then remove from heat and let cool.

2. Grease the interior of the slow cooker crock with nonstick cooking oil spray.

3. With a wire whisk, combine the flour, baking powder, baking soda, and salt in a medium bowl.

4. In a large bowl, beat the eggs and 1 cup of the sugar until thick.

continued ▶

Moroccan Golden Saffron Cake *continued* ▶

5. Add the flour mixture to the egg mixture and stir to combine well. Stir in the rosewater, 1 teaspoon of the vanilla, the dates, apricots, and walnuts.

6. Pour the batter into the prepared slow cooker. Cover with six layers of paper towels. Cook on high for 2 to 3 hours. Turn off the slow cooker, uncover, remove the paper towels, and let the cake cool for 10 minutes.

7. Meanwhile, stir the water and the remaining ¾ cup sugar in a small saucepan over medium-high heat and bring to a simmer. Reduce the heat to low and let simmer for 5 minutes, until the sugar is melted; then stir in the remaining ½ teaspoon vanilla.

8. Poke holes evenly in the cake with a toothpick or wooden skewer. Spoon the vanilla syrup over the top of the cake and then sprinkle with the chopped pistachios. Let the cake cool to room temperature.

9. To serve, cut the cake into diamond shapes, as you would for baklava.

Recipe Index

Index

CPSIA information can be obtained
at www.ICGtesting.com
Printed in the USA
LVHW060447140621
690122LV00006B/469